THAILAND
TEMPLES AND TRADITIONS

WHITE STAR PUBLISHERS

CONTENTS

TEXT
MARIA GRAZIA CASELLA

GRAPHIC DESIGN
PAOLA PIACCO

© 2007 White Star S.p.A.
Via Candido Sassone, 22/24
13100 Vercelli, Italy
www.whitestar.it

TRANSLATION: STUDIO TRADUZIONI VECCHIA, MILAN

ISBN 978-88-544-0353-6

REPRINT:
1 2 3 4 5 6   12 11 10 09 08 07

Color separation: Chiaroscuro, Turin
Printed in China

Taken from:
THAILAND
© 2004 White Star S.p.A.
ISBN 88-540-0102-3
BANGKOK - Queen of Siam
© 2005 White Star S.p.A.
ISBN 88-544-0069-6

1 The Wat Phra Boromathat in Chaiya, north of Surat Thani.

2-3 The four large chedi of the Wat Pho, Bangkok.

4-5 A beach on Phuket Island.

6-7 The Chao Phraya flows past the City of Angels.

8 top left The Wat Yai Suwannaram, in Phetchaburi.

8 top right Dancers from the Chiang Mai area.

8 bottom left The famous Karon Beach, on Phuket Island.

8 bottom right The Thailand and its nature.

9 The Wat Phra Mahathat, near Si Satchhanalai.

10-11 The Akha inhabit the hill regions

12-13 The countryside of Krabi.

14-15 Monks in front of the Buddha at Wat Ko Sirey.

THAILAND: A TROPICAL PARADISE

Mysterious and enticing, Thailand is the perfect incarnation of the "exotic dream." It is a country of age-old traditions, of flowers and smiles, of spirituality and harmony – a land that, like few others, never ceases to amaze. Heir to the ancient Kingdom of Siam, it ranges over a surface area of 215,508 sq. mi. (513,115 sq. km) – more or less the same size as France. Its shape evokes the head of an elephant, which is also the nation's symbolic animal, with the "trunk" represented by the Kra Isthmus. The narrow peninsular that thrusts southward between the Gulf of Thailand and the Indian Ocean, bordered by fantastic beaches and surrounded by a string of archipelagoes that are the very essence of a tropical Eden, is one of the country's four geographical and climatic regions. Mountainous ranges covered with forests and lush alluvial valleys typify the northern region bordering Laos

and Myanmar, with its administrative center in the city of Chiang Mai. The north, which is the cradle of Thai civilization, retains numerous artistic and cultural testimonies of the nation's history and is still peopled by nomadic mountain tribes.

Much of the northeastern region, which borders Laos and Cambodia, is occupied by the bare, arid Khorat plateau, marked by low, undulating hills. For a long time this region was isolated from the rest of the country and was strongly influenced by the Khmer culture. Furrowed by the course of the Chao Phraya (the "River of Kings") and its tributaries, the highly fertile Central Plain is the heart of the country, as well as being the richest and most productive area. Rice-fields extend across the landscape as far as the eye can see, and the region was the setting for the important events that forged the history of the nation. It was also the site of the great imperial cities of the past.

16 left In the shade of a chapel, the statue of a previous abbot of Wat Phra Boromathat awaits donations for the upkeep of the temple and to feed the poor.

16 right The cliffs of Phang Nga Bay, here shown near Krabi, are made from calcareous outcrops sculpted by the sea, which often leaves hollows within.

Recent archeological discoveries have established that what is now Thailand was already inhabited in the Bronze Age. The arrival of the Mon people, who were of Indo-Chinese origins and settled in the northwestern regions, introducing Theravada Buddhism to the area, dates back to the 9th to the 11th centuries. In 1259, with King Mengrai's ascent to the throne, the expansion of the Lanna kingdom began. Its capital was at Chiang Saen, and with the conquest of new territories, the kingdom subsequently grew to extend from the borders with Laos as far as Lamphun. The Lanna kingdom's period of prosperity lasted for over 200 years, during which the new capital Chiang Mai was founded.

Stability ended in the 15th century with the death of King Tilokaraj and the beginnings of conflict with the nearby kingdom of Sukhothai, which was considered the first-ever truly Thai dominion in history. Founded in 1238, the Sukhothai empire stretched from Lampang in the north to Vientiane in what is now Laos, and toward the south as far as the Malaysian peninsular. The Sukothai kingdom is remembered as the golden age of Thai culture; literature and the arts flourished as never before, and the foundations of the writing system from which the modern Thai alphabet derives, were laid down. The decline of Sukhothai coincided with the rise of Ayutthaya, the new capital founded by King U-Thong in 1350 on an island at the conflu-

ence of the rivers Chao Phraya, Pasak and Lopburi, at the center of a boundless expanse of paddy-fields. Ayutthaya was a very powerful city with magnificent buildings and awe-inspiring temples. In the 16th century, diplomats from Portugal, Spain, Holland, England and France made their first visits to Ayutthaya, setting up embassies there. In 1767, when at the peak of its grandeur, Ayutthaya was invaded and pillaged by the Burmese army. The Siamese built a new capital at Thonburi, on the western bank of the Chao Phraya.

This city remained the capital until 1782; then on the orders of the outstanding military leader Chakri, it was moved to the opposite side of the river, onto the artificial island of Rattanakosin. Chakri was crowned king of Siam with the name of Rama I, and was the founder of the current royal dynasty. In 1932, following a peaceful coup d'état, the Kingdom of Siam became a constitutional monarchy, which in 1939 changed its name to Thailand, "The Land of Free Men." The current sovereign, King Bhumibol Adulyadej, a direct descendant of King Rama I, ascended the throne in 1946, with the name Rama IX. He is the world's longest ruling living monarch and is loved and venerated like a demigod by all his subjects. As a constitutional monarch, he has only three "rights" – to encourage, to warn, and to be consulted – which in more than fifty years of rule have allowed him to guide his people with wisdom.

18 The Buddha in a rare "western style" seated pose emerges into the light in Wat Putthaisawan, just outside the island on which Ayutthaya stands.

19 The great prang of Wat Phra Ram towers over a decapitated statue; this was the fate of almost all the statues of the Buddha in Ayutthaya.

Thailand today has a population of over 50 million people, mostly of Thai ethnicity, 90 percent of whom are of the Buddhist faith (the State religion), followed by Hinduism and by a local form of animism. The prevailing doctrine is that of Theravada, the most ancient and traditional Buddhist school; it obliges its male followers, at least once in their lives, to undergo a period as a monk, which in some cases may continue all their lives. During the period of internship, the monks wear the typical saffron-colored robe and live in temples so that they can learn the teachings of Buddha, taking part in religious ceremonies and the daily rite of alms-seeking. For Thai people, nothing is more sacred than Buddhism and the Monarchy, and visitors are expected to show the utmost respect for these two icons of the national culture.

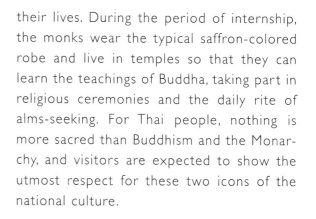

20 The most important wats, including Wat Phra Boromathat in Chaiya, near Surat Thani, have classrooms in which the novices study the usual school subjects.

21 Wat Mahatat, in Nakhon Si Thammarat, is the most important temple in southern Thailand: inside, sparkling gold enhances the many statues of the Buddha.

21 center left A worshipper of Indian origin makes an offering in a temple. The city of Trang, in the deep south, is home to Hindu, Chinese and Muslim communities.

21 bottom left Groups of novices at Wat Phra Suwannaram in Phetchaburi eat lunch in the refectory.

21 bottom right Buddhas in various mudra (symbolic poses of the body and hands) above an altar in Wat Chom Sawan, in northern Phrae.

In addition to the Thai people, other ethnic groups live in the country. The largest community is the Chinese, who settled in Thailand so long ago that they are perfectly integrated although they have maintained their own customs and traditions. In the same way, the citizens of Laotian or Khmer origins, who live mainly in the northeast, are also culturally assimilated to the Thais. The situation is different for the Muslims of Malaysian origins, who are concentrated mostly in the southern region, and for the Chao Khao, the "hill tribes," ethnic groups of Burmese, Chinese or Tibetan origin that live in the north. These population groups have kept their cultural identity practically intact, and this manifests itself in particular through a strong sense of belonging to the clan.

22 top A woman from the south, recognizable by her slight stature which is more Malaysian than typically Thai, chooses a coconut from a big pile.

22 bottom left Peasants in Sukhothai, at the northernmost limit of the central plain, tend the suan, the family vegetable-garden.

22 bottom right and 23 top left The South has a more generous climate and landscape than the North: here, the rice fields do not need terracing.

23 top right Located near waterways (or, as in this case, artificial basins) the suan produce bananas and many other kinds of tropical fruit.

22-23 In northern Thailand, these country-folk seem overdressed for a tropical climate, but they are seeking to protect themselves from the insects as well as from the sun.

24 left Famous for their custom of elongating young girls' necks with brass rings, the Padaung, a subgroup of the Karen, probably originated from Burma.

24 top right Rural houses, in this case near Mae Hong Son, are always slightly elevated to keep out snakes and other dangerous animals.

24 center right Nowadays it is not easy to see the hill tribes wearing their wonderful costumes, but the character of these peoples will nonetheless enchant observant visitors.

24 bottom right and 24-25 The protective medals that adorn the neck of this farmer from Mae Hong Son reveal his Burmese origins; the woman with the pipe, however, descends from the Chinese tribes who have settled in the region over the centuries.

In the forests between Chiang Mai and Mae Hong Son live the Lisu: originally from southern China, they are considered the "peacocks of the hills" owing to the women's highly colorful costumes, which are embellished by elegant bodices and decorated with silver jewels. The Meo, also from southern China, are one of the most open groups, much more friendly to visitors than the other communities are. It is difficult to locate the Lahu, nomadic tribes originally from Tibet who started to come into Thailand at the end of the last century and who still move quite frequently from one valley to another: their villages, which consist of dwellings built on piles, are situated quite high up. The Yao villages, spread around the Chiang Rai area, are somewhat easier to get to. The biggest community, that of the Karens, lives scattered throughout villages deep in the forests bordering with Myanmar. This tribe has the legendary "giraffe-women" with extremely long necks, adorned with gold rings. This "beauty treatment" is, however, the privilege of a few chosen girls: those who are lucky (or unlucky, depending on one's point of view) enough to have been born under a full moon. The costume of the Yao women is also truly unique; it has a kind of fluffy red boa tied tightly around the neck, and is completed by an elegant black turban. In the same area, some villages of the Akha can also be found; this is one of the poorest groups, despite the fact that men and women usually wear sumptuous silver headdresses and spectacular costumes decorated with jewels. These objects testify to the richness of the craft tradition of the northern tribes, for whom jewels are not just adornment, represent the wealth of the entire community.

26 top left For the Akha, material riches do not exist, but the people are generous and lively, as this mother and her daughter show.

26 bottom Akha women are famous for the silver ornaments that they wear, which are sought after by the other hill tribes.

26 top right Altering body proportions is still common among the hill tribes: for example, this young Padaung girl does not wear rings around her neck but has stretched earlobes.

26-27 Though her shoulders are laden with a board for transporting heavy loads, this Akha girl retains a gentle facial expression, reflecting the sweet nature for which her people are known.

Silver working is one of the main craft activities in Chiang Mai, which is considered to be one of Asia's most important artistic centers. Silversmiths' workshops are found throughout the city, with the most renowned usually clustered around the Wua Lai quarter. The silversmiths produce sophisticated vases and finely engraved ceremonial cups appreciated and sought after by collectors the world over. The delicate celadon ceramics, with their unmistakable blue-green color, also typical of the northern region and of Chiang Mai in particular, are likewise in great demand among collectors. The production method for porcelain was introduced to Chiang Mai in the 13th century by a group of about 300 Chinese ceramists who were working at the court of Sukhothai; their remarkable products were sought after throughout southeast Asia. However, silk remains Thailand's most famous and renowned handicraft product, and its manufacture has been an integral part of the country's rural culture for thousands of years. Breeding the silkworms, spinning and weaving on the loom have always been typical activities, especially in the villages of the northeast. The high-profile presence of Thai silk on the international market was strongly influenced by Jim Thompson, an American businessman who responsible for having transformed this craft activity into a true industry.

28-29 *Weaving is one of the most widely practiced and profitable craft activities for the people of the North, where silk has been produced in traditional ways for thousands of years.*

29 top *A silversmith at work in one of the many silver workshops of Chiang Mai, in the heart of the country's northern region.*

29 center *Porcelain boasts an ancient tradition; Chinese ceramists working in Sukhothai in the 13th century brought their skills to northern Thailand.*

29 bottom *Two women use wool-winders to wind up a skeins of yarn for embroidery, another important element of northern Thailand's craft products.*

30-31 *A pair of elephants confront each other on-stage during a theatrical dance performance with a historical background.*

30 bottom left *Dancing with slow, measured gestures to narrate the story, a group of actors performs in a* khon *representation taken from the Ramakien.*

30 bottom right *It is not necessary to the theater to admire costumed dancers: there is always a group performing near the Erawan Sanctuary.*

31 *Involved in a traditional performance, a dancer holding an artificial* naga *takes a step.*

Guardians of a refined, thousand-year-old culture of which they are justifiably proud, Guardians of a refined, thousand-year-old culture of which they are justifiably proud, the Thai people are real masters of the "art of living." And they do not miss the chance to show it either with the harmonious sensuality of their traditional dances or the elegance of their decorative arts, or through their appetizing and spicy gourmet cuisine, considered one of the most desirable of the Orient, or ... with a simple smile. Whether it expresses serenity of spirit, gratitude or real happiness, the smile says a lot about the Thais people's enjoyment of life, revealing a philosophy often unknown to Westerners. Sincere and spontaneous, the smile is the most genuine expression of *sanuk,* a key word in the Thai vocabulary, which means that certain "taste for enjoyment" at the base of every activity and of every action of the Thai people. There is no job, however socially prestigious and well paid, that is worth doing if it does not include at least a pinch of healthy *sanuk.* At the same time, a goodly dose of *sanuk* is what contributes to making even the most unwelcome and boring job acceptable. The maximum of *sanuk,* however, is in the convivial reunions of all members of the family, the cornerstone of Thai society. Traditionalists to the core, they are intimately and deeply connected to the own nuclear families, held to be one of the basic values for national cohesion after, needless to say, Buddhism and the monarchy. Few other Asian peoples have developed of such a taste for beauty and such a refined esthetic sense as to achieve a level of excellence recognized and appreciated throughout the world. The fullest expression of Thai art is the dance, which cannot be separated from the theater. In Thailand one always speaks of dance-theater: when the speaker indicates one of the two, the other is automatically implied. The most classical form of the dance- theater is the *khon,* whose representations are inspired by episodes taken from the *Ramakien,* the Thai version of the epic Indian drama, the *Ramayana.* The actors, who wear splendid masks embellished by decorations and brocaded costumes, move on the stage like mimes while the verses of the narrative are sung or recited by a chorus located near the orchestra.

The fixedness of the masks in reality serves to accentuate the expressiveness of their extraordinarily graceful and harmonious movements, especially those of their hands and feet. Originally performances of *khon* dance-theater lasted for over 20 hours and were produced on two consecutive days, though the entire performance of the *Ramakien* lasts for a good 720 hours. Contemporary performances of the various episodes, which are regularly given at the National Theater, at the Chalerm Krung Royal Theater and at the Thailand Cultural Center, are modern adaptations, the work of King Rama II. These performances seldom last for more than three hours. The more informal version of Thai dance-theater is the *lakhon,* in which the actors, with some exceptions, do not wear masks. Besides drawing on the *Ramakien,* the texts also draw on romantic stories and legends from the rich Thai folk tradition. The costumes are the same as those of the khon but the dance movements are more fluid and sensual. In Bangkok, groups of *lakhon* dancers perform daily around Lak Muang and the Erawan Sanctuary for the faithful who come to thank the gods for having granted their prayers. The dancers are always dressed from head to toe and accompanied by musicians, but the number of scenes and their length and complexity depend on the donations of the worshippers.

32 and 33 top left The complex gestures and dance steps — here shown at the sanctuary of Erawan in Bangkok — are coded in an "alphabet," the mae bot.

33 center left A group of young dancers performs at Chiang Mai, in Thailand's far north.

33 bottom left and top right Dressed in brocade outfits which imitate traditional courtiers' costumes, dancers perform a dance from the Ramakien.

Muay thai, the Thai style of boxing, calls for a completely different kind of movement. It is the national sport, a modern version of an ancient martial art, the origins of which have been lost in the mists of time. Indeed, from time immemorial Thai warriors have always developed a kind of body-to-body combat, which used to be the best method of defense on the dangerous battlefields of southeastern Asia. In the 16th century, on the wishes of King Naresuan the Great, a national hero and outstanding boxer, muay thai was elevated to the realm of a discipline fundamental to military training.

Each muay thai match involves five rounds of three minutes each, with breaks of two minutes, and is preceded by the wai khru, a kind of dance (also an excellent warm-up exercise) with which the athlete pays homage to his coach. Unlike western boxing, Thai boxing allows fighting using each part of the body so that, in addition to punches, kicks and blows can be delivered with arms, elbows, knees and feet. The match takes place in front of a frenzied crowd and the winner, by knockout or by points, is decided by the joint verdict of three referees. Another sport practiced throughout the country, which is decidedly less cruel, is takraw – in its popular form similar to volleyball. Takraw is a mostly spontaneous sport played everywhere. The same goes for kite-fighting, a sport very popular with Thais of all ages. These contests usually occur in March and April in order to take advantage of the light breezes of the dry season which, all over the country, are perfect for lifting kites into the sky.

34 top The engrossed expression of this athlete of muay thai, Thai boxing, is a reminder of the strong ritual component of the Thai national sport.

34 bottom Takraw, a sort of volley-ball played without using the hands, requires agility and speed.

34-35 It's difficult to visit Sanam Luang, in front of Wat Phra Kaeo, without seeing the sky dotted with kites, loved by children and adults alike.

35 bottom Multi-colored butterfly kites laid out for purchase by kite-flying enthusiasts. The activity involves true competitiveness.

36-37 At Sanam Luang, kites are a familiar sight: on the vast esplanade, a hawker displays his multicolored wares.

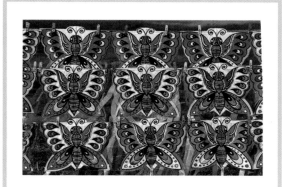

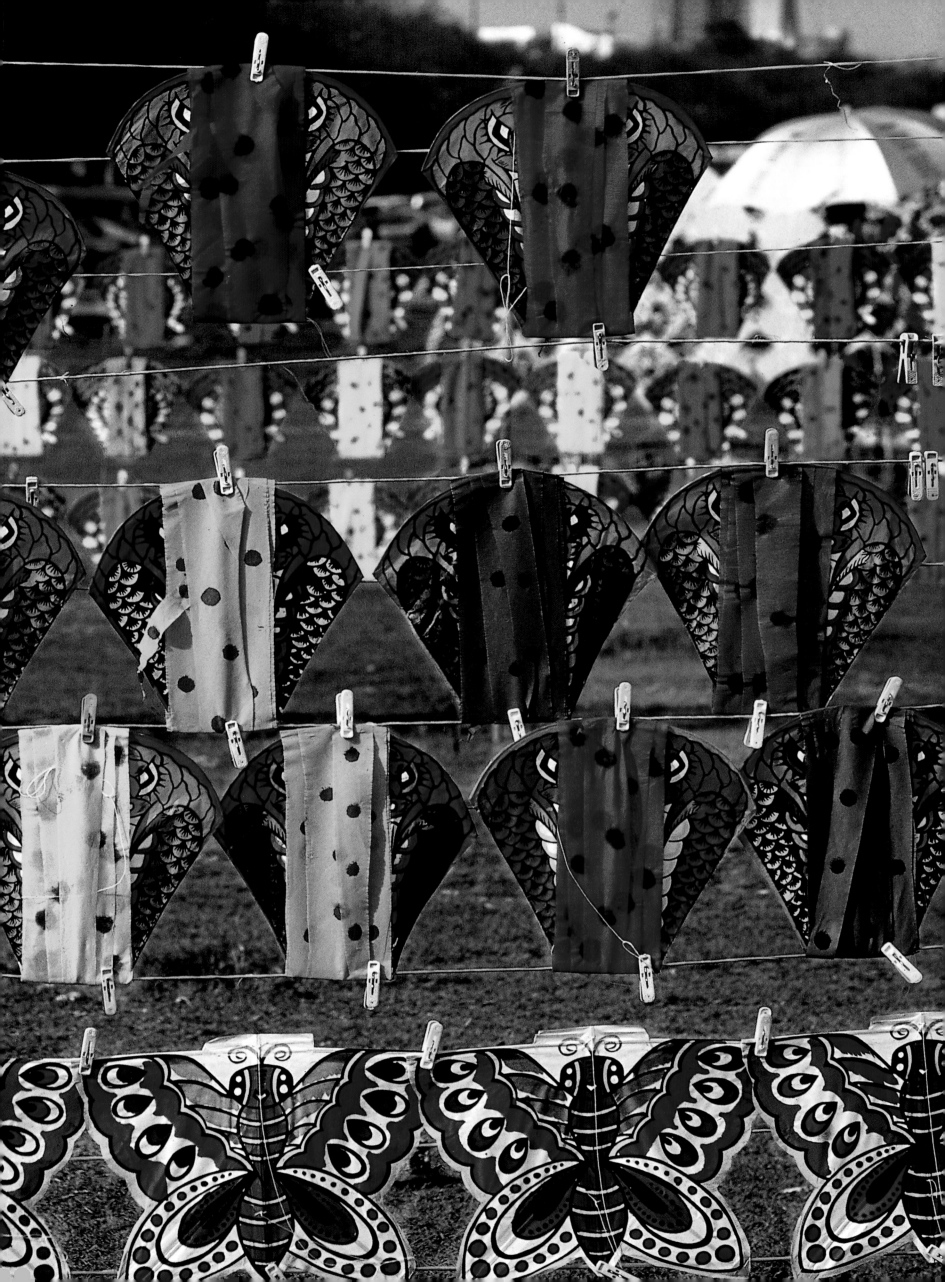

38-39 As a sign of expiation, Thais place thousands of votive offerings on the waterways during Loy Krathong.

39 top During Loy Krathong, a festival linked to the cycle of the seasons, the people of Bangkok stud the waters with thousands of flickering candles.

39 bottom left Offered to the water to thank and placate the spirits, the simplest krathong are made with banana leaves in the guise of "floaters" and then decorated with flowers.

39 bottom right Quite another spirit enlivens Songkran, the Thai New Year, when the water become a means of purification and everything is sanuksanan — amusement.

40 top and 40-41 Facing Anantasamakhom Palace (formerly the Parliament), the army band is ready to parade before the king.

41 top and center Raek-Na-Khwan (the festival of the sowing of rice) has its origins in an ancient Indian rural ceremony. At the end of the rite, the government representative who leads the sacred ox interprets the omens to predict the outcome of the harvest.

41 bottom Young visitors wearing temporary tattoos of ancient designs await the beginning of a ritual dance.

42-43 Anantanagaraj, the Royal Boat, distinguished by sacred naga serpents adorning its bow, nears Wat Phra Kaeo.

For the Thai people, any occasion is a good occasion for a party, and indeed the national calendar is full of festivals and events. These begin in April when the Thai New Year, the *Songkran* Festival, is celebrated throughout the country with religious ceremonies and public festivities and, especially, with great water battles fought in a spirit of joy and well-wishing. In Bangkok, the place chosen by tradition for this unusual ritual is the broad esplanade of Sanam Luang, near the Grand Palace, where

marks the official beginning of the rice-planting season. The ceremony is conducted by an important Ministry of Agriculture representative, who wears a traditional costume. According to popular belief, the complete success of this complex ceremony is a good omen of an abundant harvest. Also connected to the cycle of the seasons is *Loy Krathong,* a highly atmospheric festival celebrated on the night of the full moon of the twelfth lunar month, which coincides with the end of the

the venerated statue of the Phra Buddha Sihing is transported for the occasion, which the devout then literally soak with buckets of water. At the same time, not far away, in the Wisutkasat area, Miss Songkran is elected. At the beginning of May, the Thais celebrate *Visakha Puja,* the most important of all the recurrences in the Buddhist world. It marks the birth, the enlightenment and the death of the Buddha. The faithful meet in temples to listen to the monks' sermons and, at sunset, at the end of the rites, candlelight processions occur in the sacred places. In mid-May, the Sanam Luang is the setting for the Royal Ceremony of Plowing, an ancient Brahmin ritual reintroduced by King Bhumibol Adulyadej in 1960; it

rainy season. The high point of this event is the expiation ceremony during which millions of banana-leaf boats, with flowers, candles and coins on them, are floated on water of the rivers and canals. Ratchadamnoen Avenue and the area around the Grand Palace are festively draped with flags on August 12th in honor of the birthday of Queen Sirikit. Light-and-sound shows and parades celebrate the anniversary of King Bhumibol Adulyadej, the longest reigning of the world's living monarchs. Both the king and the queen participate some days later in the military parade, the Trooping of the Colors, which is held at the Royal Palace in front of the equestrian monument of King Chulalongkorn.

Only twenty years ago almost no one outside of Thailand knew about its rich, tasty cuisine. In just a couple of decades, it has earned respect at tables throughout the world and is now appreciated from Paris to New York. The merit for its great success is the high nutritional value of its traditional dishes and especially of that unique, harmonious mixture of different flavors (spicy, salty, sour and sweet) that characterize each dish. What's more, Thai cuisine not only captivates the taste but also involves all the senses with its inviting aromas and with the elegant presentation of every single dish. Last but not least, the knowledgeable use of aromatic herbs and spices adds healthy properties to this cuisine that contribute to creating a sense of well-being in those who enjoy it. The result of a thousand-year-old tradition, handed down from generation to generation, the Thai cuisine is essentially a domestic art that reflects the lifestyle and culture of the country. The only exception is the "Royal Cuisine," a more sumptuous and refined version of the original, in the past only used in the Royal Palace and reserved for the fortunate palates of kings and their aristocratic guests. The special attribute of the Royal Cuisine was the spectacular presentation of the various dishes. For example, vegetables and fruits were literally sculpted into unusual forms and used as decorations. These were truly artistic creations, which today are the norm in the most luxurious restaurants in Bangkok and elsewhere. The basic ingredient of the Thai menu is rice, of which Thailand is one of the world's major producers. A large bowl of this grain always dominates the center of the table both on great occasions and in frugal homemade meals. To crown it, the contents of other dishes are placed on top of the rice, to offer a balanced and complete selection of tastes, flavors and preparations. Besides rice, a typical Thai meal may include the classic *tom yum kung* (sweet and sour shrimp soup) *kang khieu wan kai* (curried chicken); *kang masaman* (curried veal); *plaa phad* (fried fish); and *phad thai* (noodles) - in reality rice vermicelli fried in the Thai style.

In the Thai cuisine, great importance is placed on the spices and aromas. Unrivalled dominance goes to the hot pepper, which is found in Bangkok markets in a dozen varieties that differ from one another in taste and in potency. The most explosive and sought after is the smallest, yellow-orange one called *prig khee nu*. Equally indispensable are cumin seeds *(yira)*, nutmeg *(loog junn)*, cardamam *(grawan)*, cloves *(garn plu)*, cinnamon *(ob choei)*, curry *(pong kari)*, dry hot pepper *(prig haeng)*, sesame seeds *(nga)* and saffron *(ya faran)*. Then not to be forgotten are the roots (especially ginger and coriander), coconut milk *(kathi)*, with which curries, soups, sauces and sweets are mixed. It goes without saying that the appropriate combination of all these ingredients is a knowledgeable and refined art in which Thais have achieved undisputed levels of excellence.

The Thais are also real masters in the art of carving fruits and vegetables to make astonishing decorations for their dishes. With a few deft movements of the knife, a humble carrot or cucumber becomes a rose or chrysanthemum, a fish or a fantastic animal while a watermelon, in the hands of a true artist, can even be transformed, like magic, into a peacock.

44-45 Skilled in the use of woks and other large pans, two cooks prepare a soup of soy sprouts, shellfish and vegetables.

44 bottom left In addition to fresh fish, the markets offer various species from herring to skate, smoked or dried.

44 bottom right The mantis shrimp lined up on the rim of this bowl are part of the recipe for tom yam, one of the most famous Thai dishes.

BANGKOK, THE CITY OF ANGELS

For its inhabitants, Bangkok is and always will be *Krung Thep*, the City of Angels, a name that that evokes the times in which the capital of modern Thailand was the center of the kingdom of Siam. The city built on water pulsed with colonial charm. It was an irresistible attraction for adventurers and writers, such as Joseph Conrad and Somerset Maugham, in search of an exotic atmosphere. Nowadays those who expect to find that world unchanged will be somewhat – but not entirely – disappointed. Bangkok with its 12 million inhabitants is a megalopolis, among the most animated, chaotic and productive in all of Asia. The political, cultural and religious fulcrum of the country, it is a puzzle, which, at first glance, seems difficult to solve. In the city, fitting together perfectly are futuristic skyscrapers and ancient buildings; Buddhist temples that are oases of mysticism and flamboyant red-light districts; and modern shopping centers that are hymns to consumerism and floating markets that seem to come out of an old print. All this is found against a backdrop of tranquil tropical gardens and the most exasperating traffic imaginable.

46 top left The gleaming Gaysorn Center towers above a modern kiosk reflecting traditional design.

46 top right The image of the much-loved royal couple stands out on the Democracy Monument.

46-47 and 47 left The modern commercial city may seem to crowd out the "romantic" Bangkok of former times but, at the ground level, the seductiveness of the City of Angels still exists.

47 top right The Bot, or monastic ordination center, at the Wat Samphraya temple complex.

47 bottom right Futuristic Bangkok's latest arrival, the Sky Train reduces traffic in the capital.

48 top The graceful Anandhasamakhom palace is not typically Thai in style but is nevertheless very pleasing to the eye; it was built by King Rama V Chulallongkorn (who reigned from 1868 to 1910) and today it is the venue for important royal and State celebrations.

48 center and bottom Bangkok grows bigger each day; but a cheerful eclecticism lightens up even the most imposing towers in the central areas east of the Chao Praya.

49 Impenetrable and alluring, a glass façade contains the wonder world of the Gaysorn Center, which is considered to be the capital's trendiest shopping center.

50-51 This view offers a panorama over the beating heart of Bangkok, near Siam Square.

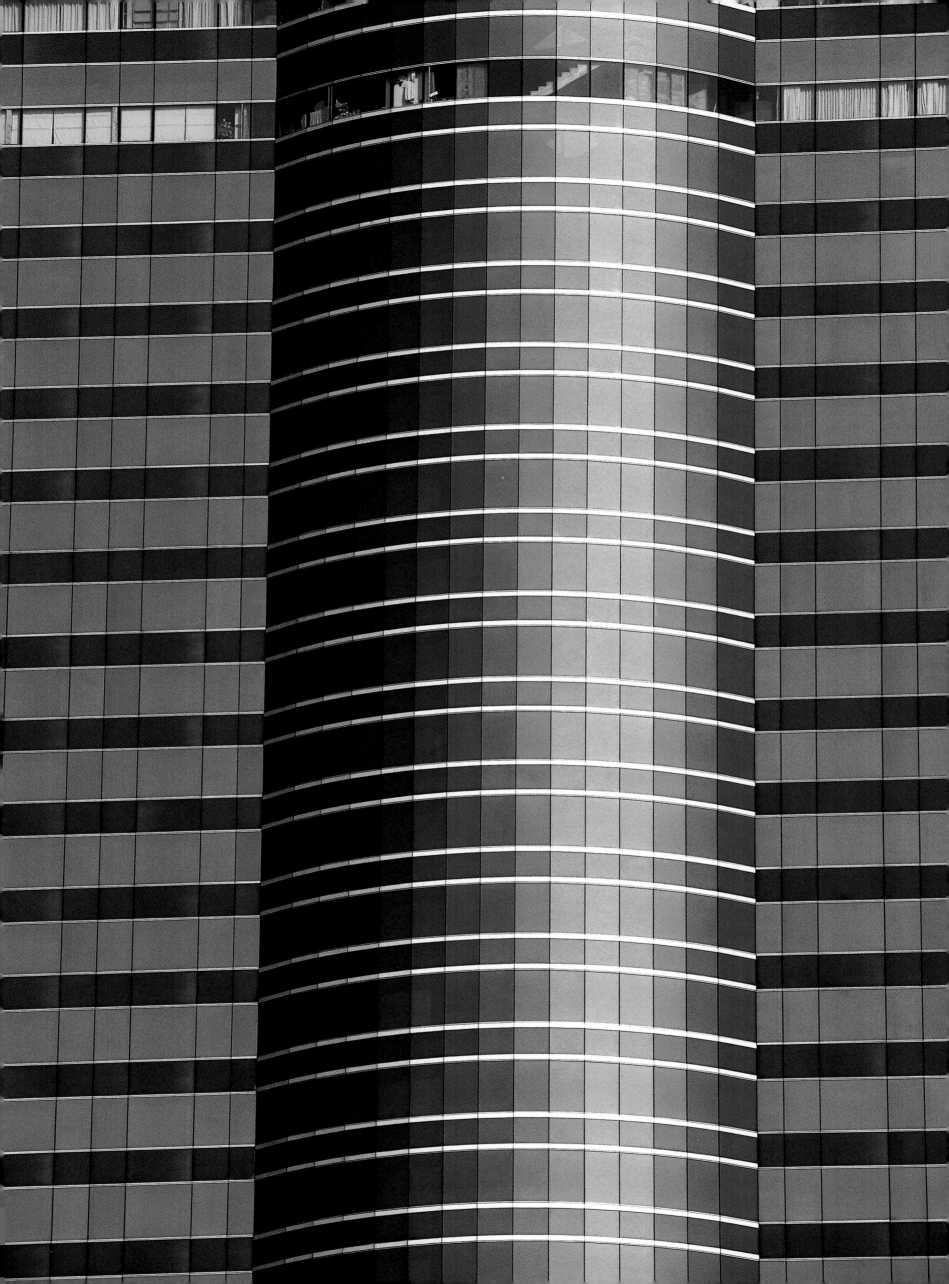

52 top left The Chakri dynasty is very much alive in the hearts of the Thais; Rama III, a sovereign with a strong character, was able to ensure his country's well-being in the early 1800s.

52 top right To define a city like Bangkok as "busy" is an understatement: the city swarms with life at all hours of the day and most of the night.

52 center and bottom Despite their perennial liveliness, Bangkok's residents find quiet moments: here (top) two locals play checkers, a popular pastime. City traffic is horrendous, but people on stalled buses seem immune to chaos and lost hours.

52-53 Bangkok youth takes eagerly to new trends, dances included. For Thais, agility and physical fitness are among their traditional values.

54 top The ubiquitous "rot tuk tuk," a speedy, inexpensive and fun form of public transport, are one of the typical features of Bangkok "at ground level."

54 bottom left The spectacular tangles of pillars and the monorail's tracks dodge the city center's heavy traffic.

54 bottom right The endless lines of vehicles at the traffic lights seem discouraging; however, with a little Eastern patience, everything flows smoothly and without accidents.

55 The picture shows the well-loved King Bhumibol Adulyadei, who was crowned with the dynastic name of Rama IX.

56-57 and 56 bottom Dusk falls quickly in Bangkok; at the 14° latitude north; the city typically has almost imperceptible seasonal variations of daylight.

57 right Thanon Phloenchit demonstrates Bangkok's highway congestion. Low-fare taxis (yellow, green, red and blue) now compete with private cars in terms of numbers.

58 Bangkok lives both day and night and is always splendidly lit up: here, a noodle shop's sign cajoles the appetite of the evening clientele.

59 From dusk till dawn, the city lives parallel lives in the various areas invaded by the farang: from Thanon Khao San to Patpong, these crowded worldly paradises are full of pubs and fashionable discos, restaurants, shops and gyms showing muay thai (Thai boxing) all open to foreigners.

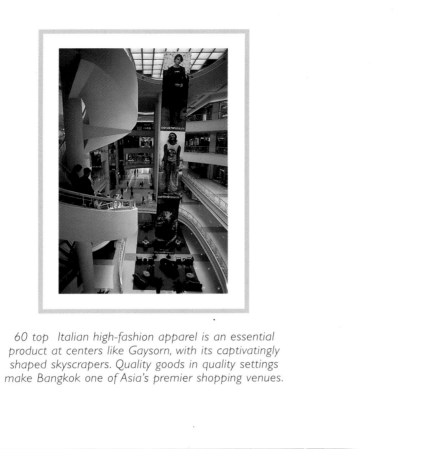

60 top Italian high-fashion apparel is an essential
product at centers like Gaysorn, with its captivatingly
shaped skyscrapers. Quality goods in quality settings
make Bangkok one of Asia's premier shopping venues.

60 center, bottom and 60-61 The Siam Discovery
Center (above) and the WTC (below and on the right)
are frightening iceboxes with excessive air-
conditioning, but their futuristic architecture and
interiors exert a fascination.

Despite being a concentration of Thai history and culture, Bangkok is a relatively young city. It was founded a little over 200 years ago, after the Burmese captured Ayutthaya, the ancient Thai capital. The new capital was first located at Thonburi, on the western bank of the Chao Phraya river, where it remained for fifteen years, until 1782. At that time Chakri, a young army general, was crowned king of Siam with the name of Rama. Chakri had won the esteem of the population by recapturing in Laos the Emerald Buddha, a statue of incalculable spiritual value for Buddhists. Rama, who was the founder of the current royal dynasty, decided to transfer the capital to the other side of the river, onto an artificial island that he called Rattanakosin: "the place in which the Emerald Buddha reposes."

Even now Rattanakosin is the city's monumental and ceremonial heart. Here are found the immense Royal Palace complex and Wat (temple) Phra Kaeo, the country's major Buddhist temple, a kind of Thai Vatican. Over the centuries the city has extended beyond measure, undergoing a radical urban transformation, especially during the second half of the 20th century, which was a boom period in Thailand's economic, social and cultural life.

Rattanakosin Island continues to be the capital's main tourist attraction, though royal life goes on elsewhere. Even the king no longer lives in the Grand Palace, having moved his residence to Chitralada Palace in the elegant new residential quarter of Dusit. With its tree-lined boulevards bordered by government buildings, it is the equal of a European capital. It was not accidental that the new royal district built at the beginning of the last century was constructed on the orders of King Rama V; he was first sovereign to have traveled in the West, and brought back plans and innovative ideas for modernizing Bangkok.

62-63 A monochromatic prang stands out next to the Aphonphimok Pavilion and the Dusit Throne Room in the Grand Palace.

62 bottom left The Dusit Throne Room (late 1700s) is a Rattnakosin masterpiece, an evocation of the magnificent architecture of Ayutthaya, the former capital sacked by the Burmese army in 1757.

62 bottom right The 19th-century neoclassical-style Chakri Maha Prasat built from a design by John Chinitz, a Briton.

63 A band leads the precision changing of the guard at the Grand Palace, the magnificent and highly ornate royal complex in Bangkok.

64 top left European-style statues, depicting armored spear throwers, support the lamps in a corridor of the Chakri Maha Prasat.

64 top right Under the canopy of the Audience Room in the Chakri Maha Prasat, the king receives the credentials of foreign ambassadors.

64 bottom left In the Dusit Audience Room, magnificent inlays of mother-of-pearl ornament the teak of the sumptuous throne of Rama I, founder of Bangkok.

64 bottom right and 64-65 European-style furniture and décor in the Grand Palace is a simple concession to the exotic, as this reception room demonstrates.

Bangkok's Chinatown is marked by frenetic business activity which continues far into the night. Yaowarat Road, the backbone of this quarter, is also known as the "Street of Gold" because of its high concentration of jewelry shops.

Around it is a maze of alleys with Chinese herb shops, stands, ideogram writers, and ethnic restaurants.

66 top and bottom right Bangkok's Chinese are mainly involved in business, from food supplies to jewelry.

66 center left Prepared foods on sale in Chinatown: the cuisine is a crossover between Chinese and Thai tastes.

66 center right Spiny durian with their intense aroma are on display in a shop in Bangkok's Chinatown.

66 bottom left A Chinese pharmacy: allopathic medicines are on the right; numerous traditional remedies are on the left.

67 The lit signs of Thanon Yaowarat, Chinatown's Street of Gold may display either Chinese characters or syllabic Thai writing.

68 top left The Phra Sumane tower, part of
Bangkok's fortifications, dominates this section of the
Chao Phraya's eastern bank.

68 top right An elegant pavilion-pier on the
river reflects the graceful forms of palatial
architecture.

In contrast to so much frenzy, the colonial quarter, which extends along the banks of the Chao Phraya offers a decisively more relaxing atmosphere. This is the ideal place to go in search of literary memories, following in the footsteps of the writers who stayed at the Oriental Hotel, which, in its oldest wing, preserves its Authors' Lounge unchanged. Here, amidst old photographs and rattan chairs, the rite of high tea is celebrated in the most perfect British style. Traces of the colonial era

ancient capital, was also founded on the water. To gain an idea of how the Venice of the Orient appeared to travelers at the beginning of the century, go to the right bank of the Chao Phraya and enter the heart of the old quarter built on a web of canals (klongs), where the characteristic "long-tailed" boats ply. As you gradually go farther and farther away from visitors' routes, you discover the other face of Bangkok with its old wooden houses, dwellings built on piles,

also emerge in the buildings of the East Asiatic Company, the legendary Company of the Indies, one of the first western businesses established in the city. The edifice is reflected in the calm waters of Chao Phraya, "the River of Kings," from time immemorial the country's main artery, along which cities and businesses flower.

It was not by chance that Thonburi, the

small Buddhist temples, a world in which the noise and rhythms of the metropolis seem to belong to another reality.

This world was almost entirely isolated until 1932. Then the old quarter was connected to the new city with the opening of the Memorial Bridge, built to celebrate the first 150 years of the Chakri dynasty and the founding of Bangkok.

68 bottom Smiling families and quiet, flower-graced
corners: this is the rule along Bangkok's canals such
as the Khlong Khaen shown here, where wood holds
its own over cement.

68-69 A variety of passenger boats ply the Chao
Phraya; they provide an excellent alternative to driving
through the suffocating streets.

70 top With expert skill, a woman makes garlands, a hand-made product always in demand among Bangkok's residents The highly perfumed garlands symbolize both the beauty of Buddhist doctrine and human frailty They are usually offered in temples or placed on altars.

70-71 Chinese-style umbrellas protect the stands of the innumerable peddlers who dot the streets of Bangkok.

71 top In Bangkok's central area, each quarter has a commercial association; the shops near Golden Mountain, for example, offer cult articles of every type and size.

71 bottom Frozen seafood has no place in the Thai diet; every market offers fresh fish and shellfish at affordable prices.

If a cruise among the Thonburi *klongs* has the power to evoke the authentic spirit of the old Thai capital, the people's markets reveal the city's true nature. Not without reason, Bangkok's markets are considered to make up the largest bazaar in Southeast Asia, a place where it is possible to find practically anything. Customers just have to know where to look. Even though luxurious shopping centers have popped up nearly everywhere in recent years, the markets continue to exercise an irresistible attraction. The most famous, as well as the largest and best attended, is the Chatuchak Market, with something like 6,000 stalls, held on the weekends in the park of the same name in the city's northern section. An unlimited labyrinth of goods, perfumes and colors, it is where the seeker finds everything and more. An entire day is barely enough to visit the various sections (clothing, food, flowers, fruit, housewares, etc.). However, it is generally the Indo-Chinese artisan and antique areas that attract attention, with their kioks full of rattan chests and traditional ceramics, silver jewelry, musical instruments, lacquered objects and precious silks. An ample (and controversial) section of the market is reserved for the sale of domestic and wild animals. Nowadays it is rather unusual to see tiger pups or gigantic cobras for sale as this is forbidden by the authorities, but it is possible to buy, in addi-

tion to the traditional pets, the terrible fighting cocks and Siamese fish of which the Thais are true connoisseurs.

The sweet perfume of oriental essences will guide visitors' steps toward the Pak-Klong-Talad Market, the city's most popular flower market, where for a few *bahts,* they buy fabulous orchid shoots, Thailand's floral symbol, and traditional garlands of jasmine. Exotic plants and flowers, this time in vases, are the specialty of Thewet Market, whose stalls are a real joy to the botanists, astonished by the extraordinary number and variety of rare species on offer. Another popular market is Lang Krasuang, a sort of flea market held near the Ministry of the Interior, where you can find all kinds of second-hand objects from old typewriters to electrical apparatus and used clothing of every style.

But Woeng Nakhon Kasem, the legendary Thieves' Market, is by far the most curious and fascinating bazaar, although the times are now a distant memory when art dealers from nearly everywhere combed through its stalls. Then people got fabulous deals by discovering authentic Khmer antiques and objets d'art of incalculable value offered for very little money. However, this market still continues to be a reliable source for unusual, tasteful purchases, among which are porcelains, old inlaid mother-of-pearl furniture, and more or less antique objects from all over Indochina.

72 and 72-73 The markets delight the eye and the nose: heaps of fresh products — fruit and vegetables but also flower garlands to take to temples — arrive in the city each day from the surrounding countryside.

74-75 and 75 Retail trade takes place daily and all over Bangkok: the shops, boutiques and simple stalls, always lively, are not just where buying and selling occurs, but where life itself is played out.

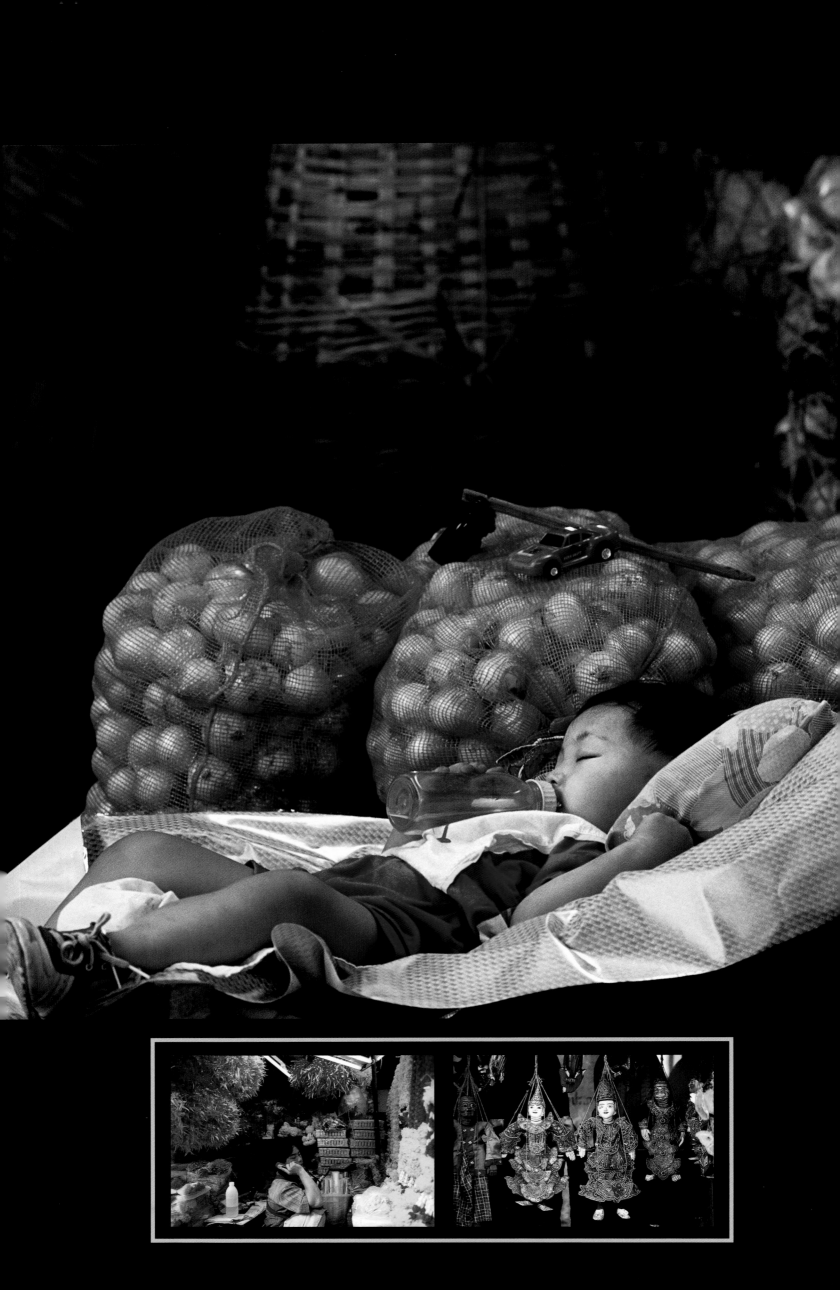

"GIVE FREEDOM TO THE BIRDS
AND
GOOD LUCK AND HAPPINESS
WILL BE WITH YOU ALWAYS
90 B"

76 top left At Lumphini Park, athletic bodies cast in bronze evoke the enthusiasm that the Thais devote to exercising in Bangkok's green areas.

76 top right Queen Sirikit is portrayed in a gilded sculpture at the entrance to Benchasiri Park, which was created to celebrate her 60th birthday.

76-77 One of the lakes in Lumphini Park that invitingly extend to the feet of the army of towers that dominate Bang Rak, the modern heart of the city.

77 top Lumphini Park is the perfect place to escape from the chaos of the city. Though always very busy, quiet reigns everywhere.

*77 bottom People of all ages spontaneously form
groups in Lumphini Park to involve themselves in the
cadenced movements of tai-chi-chuan.*

In contrast to the excited confusion of the markets is the quiet of the parks and gardens, though, to tell the truth, green oases in the heavily trafficked and chaotic city of Bangkok are a rarity. However, in compensation, they are well cared for and much used by the population. The city's green "lung" is Chatuchak Park, adjacent to the market of the same name; it is, therefore, the best place to recover after a day of shopping.

Lumphini Park, which takes its name from the Nepalese place where the Buddha was born, is the oldest and best loved park, visited from the early hours of the morning, when it is transformed into an open-air gym. In the shade of its trees, Thais gather by the hundreds for an exercise hour that involves, depending on inclination and age, the rhythm of aerobic dance or the calm movements of tai-chi-chuan, the traditional Chinese form of gymnastics.

During the course of the day, the park becomes the meeting place for chess players, who gather in the shade of the pagodas and pavilions that dot the landscape. The park's two lakes, populated by fish and turtles, are criss-crossed by people in pedal boats.

The vast green area of Sanam Luang, also known as the Kings' Field, extends to the north of the Grand Palace. In addition to being a popular evening meeting place for the capital's inhabitants, it is the background for official celebrations and ceremonies. For example, the solemn rituals for the cremation of Thai kings occur here, as well as traditional festivals and New Year celebrations. The small temple on the south side of Sanam Luang is called Lak Muang. It contains the horoscope of Bangkok cast by the court astrologers at the time the capital was founded. All Thai cities have one where, according to tradition, the spirits that protect the place reside.

Also in the vicinity of the Royal Palace is Saranrom Park, once the private garden of Saranrom Palace. It is dotted with monuments, among them one to Queen Sunantha Kumarirat, the consort of King Rama V. Two green areas in Bangkok have recently been dedicated to contemporary sovereigns.

These are Benchasiri Park, small but delightfully designed, which was inaugurated on the present Queen Sirikit's 60th birthday, and the 200-acre King Rama IX Royal Park, which includes a botanic garden and a building that hosts an exhibition about the king's life and works. Amporn Park, part of the gardens of the Chitralada Palace (the current royal residence) is by far the most beautiful and evocative of Bangkok's parks and is open to the public. Among the park's tree-lined avenues, rare plants and small lakes, are the Pavilion of the Throne Room, Vimanmek Palace, and Dusit Zoo, which has various rare exotic animals, such as the Komodo monitor lizard (or Komodo dragon), the largest reptile on earth.

In 1932, the powerful kingdom of Siam became a constitutionalmonarchy. In 1939, it changed its name to Thailand, which means "The Land of Free Men." Nevertheless the king continues to be loved and venerated as a demi-god by all his subjects. A direct descendent of King Rama I, King Bhumibol Adulyadej ascended the throne in 1946 with the name Rama IX. This dynasty has had greater longevity than any previous Thai dynasty, and it is probably also the most respected in that the king is not only considered the king of the Thais but the king for the Thais, whose aspirations, desires and needs he knows. As a constitutional monarch, he has only three "rights": to encourage, to warn, and to be consulted. For the more than fifty years of his reign the king has wisely guided and helped his people and his government, even in the most difficult moments in the country's history. King Rama I decided to build a new royal palace since the one constructed at Thonburi on the Chao Phraya's western bank was threatened by erosion.

Upon precise indications from the court astrologers, work on the new complex began at 6:45 on 21 April 1782, on the artificial island of Rattanakosin. This land was obtained by the king's order through opening a defensive canal 4.5 miles (7 km) long, now called Klong Bang Lamphu and Klong Ong Ang that split the river to the north of the city and reunited it to the south.

On the inside of the canal, a strong wall over 10 feet (3 m) high and 6.5 feet (2 m) broad was raised. It was punctuated by 16 gates and 16 blockhouses, two of which are still visible today, along with a short section of the original wall. The current citadel is a splendid complex of buildings and pavilions from various eras in different styles scattered over an area of approximately 60 acres (24 hectares); it is the result of repeated additions, restorations and improvements wrought by different kings over the course of centuries. The original heart of the palace is Phra Maha Monthien, which was completed just in time for the coronation of King Rama I – and was subsequently the setting for the sumptuous investiture ceremonies for all the Chakri dynasty sovereigns. In the main building are the royal apartments. Tradition demands that every new sovereign must spend the first night of his reign in the apartments, signaling his solidarity with his predecessors and proving that he is assuming not only the honor but also the burdens and responsibilities toward the nation that his role presupposes. In this wing of the palace, only the Phra Thinang Amarin Winichai is currently open to the public.

78 The splendid Phra Sri Rattana Chedi in Wat Phra Kaeo stands in front of the spiral Mondop Library and the prang of the Royal Pantheon.

79 Dominated by the Phra Sri Rattana, this image includes three types of Buddhist monument: a chedi in the foreground, a mondop in the center, and a prang in the background.

This is the Throne, or Audience, Room where, in the days of absolute monarchy, the most important state functions were held. Diplomats on official visits came here, and the king discussed affairs of state with his ministers and counselors. Now the Throne Room is used only for the king's birthday celebrations. Another magnificent throne, a true masterpiece embellished by mother-of-pearl decoration, is in the Dusit Maha Prasat, the original Audience Room that King Rama ordered to be built, in the purest Siamese style. The building is shaped like a cross and covered by a roof of several layers painted red, green and gold, traditional Thai colors. The build-

ing culminates in a gilded *mongkut,* a spire that echoes the form of the royal crown and symbolizes the thirty-three Buddhist levels of perfection. The room is still used as a mortuary chapel for members of the royal family who have passed away. Their bodies are embalmed and can be viewed until the day arrives (and it might be months later) that the court astrologers feel is most auspicious for cremation. In great contrast to Dusit Maha Prasat, which is built in strict Siamese style, is the Chakri Maha Prasat complex. This was built in 1882 at the command of the progressive King Rama V, who made it his residence.

80 Once the enemy demons of the religion, the yaksas converted to the Buddhist doctrine and now guard the sacred temple doors, in this case, at Wat Phra Kaeo.

81 top According to popular imagination, the yaksas of the various temples, monstrous and benign, fight epic battles among themselves.

81 bottom left The faithful apply leaves of precious gold as a sign of homage to effigies of the Buddha, quite often already gilded and sometimes made of pure gold.

81 bottom right The interiors of the wats are islands of peace that would seem impossible in Bangkok. The approach to the temples must be respectful, and clothes should be modest and comfortable.

82-83 Beneath a multitude of prangs, a pair of gilded kinnaras enhances a terrace near the Grand Palace.

84 top The Grand Palace brings together examples of the purest Thai architecture.

84 bottom Red, green and gold, Thailand's traditional colors, recur in the roofs of the Grand Palace.

85 The Royal Pantheon, a visible manifestation of the concept of the divinity of kings, is open only on special occasions, such as celebrations of the Chakri dynasty.

86 and 87 The guards at the temple entrances are truly impressive, due to both their size (they stand around 27 ft tall) and the highly detailed work on their armor, which is covered in innumerable colored ceramic tiles.

88 top left A series of variously-colored yaksas support a gilded chedi of Prasat Phra Thepidon.

88 top right The "claw" represents a chofa or sky bow, a mythical bird whose shape seems derived from an extreme stylization of the Indian garuda.

88-89 This kinnari or Apsonsi stands guard within the walls of Wat Phra Kaeo.

The result is a royal palace that is, to say the least, eclectic, combining Italian neoclassical elements with oriental pagodas to the point that it immediately received as a nickname "the farang (a Western building) with a Thai hat." The hat in question was the three *mondops*, the gilded and richly worked spires that crown the roof. In them are kept the ashes of the kings, queens and princes of the Chakri dynasty. Among the eleven edifices that King Rama V built and which originally made up this wing of the Grand Palace, is the Interior Palace, in which the officials and ladies of the harem lived. In reality, this was a city with its own shops, police corps and court of justice, as well as being the home of the king's wives, the princesses, the concubines, their children and the aristocratic young ladies who attended the royal school.

In Phra Mondop, the library, is the original copy of the Gold Royal Edition of the *Tripitaka*, the sacred Buddhist scripture on which the country's religion is based. The manuscript, housed in a desk studded with mother-of-pearl standing on a carpet woven of pure silver, is in a chapel reached by four stairways and doors. Guarding it are four pairs of menacing statues of demons. Because of their perfect proportions, they are considered masterpieces of Rattanakosin craftsmanship. The Major Stupa, erected by King Rama IV on the model of the three stupas in the Royal Chapel of the ancient capital, Ayutthaya, is covered with splendid mosaics from Italy. It holds sacred relics of the Buddha. Prasat Phra Thep Bidon ("the Sanctuary of the Celestial Ancestors") is the Royal Pantheon, where life-size statues of all the Chakri dynasty kings are preserved. Under a long colonnade, you can also admire an imposing series of 178 frescoes, an 18th-century work executed by Rattanakosin artisans. These frescoes illustrate the entire cycle of the *Ramakien*, the Thai version of the *Ramayana*, India's world-famous epic poem, the verses of which are sculpted in the columns that support the gallery.

90 and 90-91 The big temple complexes such as Wat Phra Kaeo are exciting to visit, not least due to the complete lack of uniformity and the unpredictability that typifies them. Symmetry exists, but it is merely a convention: so "modest" statues of the Enlightened in soft rock (top) sit impressively alongside glittering kinnaras and golden apsonsis (left), mythical half-bird half-human creatures and newsstands guarded by sacred elephants (right) do not go unnoticed, but turn up unexpectedly in this forest of spires, kiosks and ritual pools.

92-93 In Wat Phra Khaeo, winged Garudas almost blend in with the richly detailed base of the chedi that they are protecting.

94-95 Kranok decorations, inspired from lotus, loom over this pediment in Wat Phra Kaeo.

95 Of Hindu origin, like the yaksas, the kroots or garudas in Thailand symbolize royal power.

96 top The Emerald Buddha, is Thailand's most revered and most powerful image.

96 center and bottom left The arcade encircling Wat Phra Kaeo is decorated with 178 images illustrating the

Ramakien. The two images here present the demon Tosakan (top) and the monkey-god Hanuman.

96 bottom right This scene from the Ramakien shows good King Rama seated at court.

96-97 The horrendous Tosakan, demonic king of Sri Lanka shown in this detail of the Ramakien in Wat Phra Kaeo, has only one head; his name means "ten hills" ... and an equal number of heads.

98-99 Always crowded with visitors during the day, the Wat Phra Kaeo-Grand Palace complex manifests its purest beauty at night.

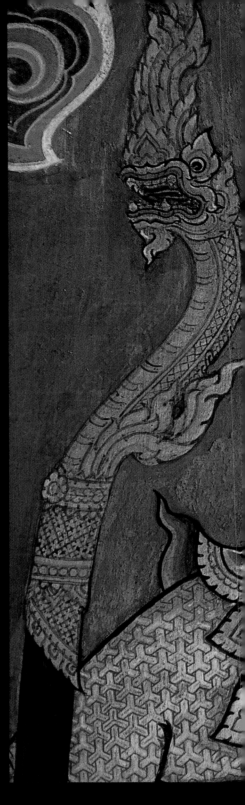

THE TEMPLES OF BANGKOK

Near the Royal Palace is Wat Pho, Bangkok's largest and oldest temple complex, comprising about one hundred buildings originally from the 16th century but which were almost entirely reconstructed by King Rama I in 1781. Within the main building (erected in 1832) is the gigantic reclining Buddha, a statue 150 feet (46 m) long and 50 feet (15 m) high, entirely covered in gold. It represents the god in the position of the *Parinibbana*, the post-mortem Nirvana. Fragments of mother-of-pearl decorate the soles of the feet, designating the 108 special attributes of the Buddha. Four large pagodas commemorate the first three kings of the Chakri dynasty (two *chedi* [pagoda-like structures]are dedicated to King Rama III). The chapels are connected by an arcade populated with about a hundred statues of the Buddha, the largest collection of its kind in all of Thailand. Besides being an important sanctuary, Wat Pho is also considered a center of secular studies, so much so that it considered "the most important university in Thailand," where traditional disciplines, such as astronomy, literature, meditation and the art of Thai massage, are studied.

100 top The enormous roof of the Great Bot looks down on the Wat Pho complex, the oldest in Bangkok and the largest in Thailand.

100 bottom left A marvelous view of the chedi spires covered with millions of fragments of multicolored ceramics. Because of the smog, they have to be periodically cleaned and polished.

100 bottom center and right Many of the cement statues that fill the Wat Pho's courtyards reached Thailand as ballast on ships that later left filled with rice.

101 Among the four magnificent major chedis in Wat Pho, the central and oldest one contains the remains of the image of the most sacred Buddha of Ayutthaya, the city destroyed by the Burmese.

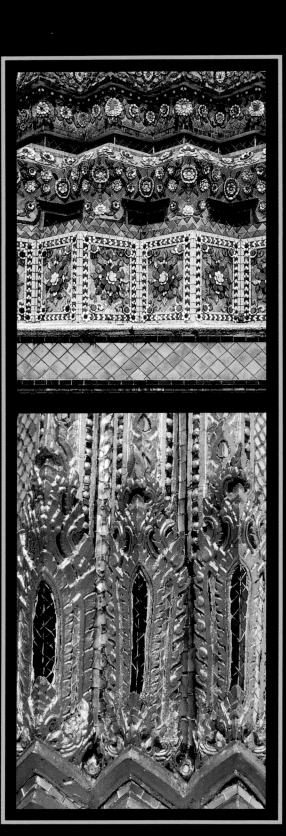

102 The incredible amount of detail creates a spectacular microcosm at Wat Pho, a world of colored geometry that remains just as complex as the visual scale widens.

102-103 The grandiose sacred Thai architecture managed an impressive masterpiece with the roofs above the main Bot of Wat Pho: in real life, the effect is no less stunning than in this view.

104 Made from a core of plastered and gilded brick, this 150-foot (45-m) long statue of the reclining Buddha in Wat Pho almost entirely occupies the vihara in which it has been placed.

105 top and center The smile of the reclining Buddha (top) measures 16.5 feet (5 m) from one corner of the mouth to the other. Spirals of mother-of-pearl (center) mimic the wrinkles in the skin on the soles of the feet.

105 bottom left The statue of the Buddha in meditation venerated in the Great Bot in Wat Pho was saved from the ruins of Ayutthaya in 1767.

105 bottom right This statue, with cheeks and the eyelids decorated by gold leaves applied by worshippers, is part of the procession of Seated Buddhas in the Great Bot.

106 Thonburi, which for fifteen years following the fall
of Ayutthaya was Thailand's capital, is located Chao
Phraya's western banks and is dominated by the
majestic prang of Wat Arun.

107 top Amid the four prangs that mark the corners
of Wat Arun, or Temple of the Dawn, arise an equal
number of mondops, distinguishable from the chedi
because they rise from square bases.

Another center of advanced study is the prestigious Mahachulalongkorn Buddhist University, located in Wat Mahathat. It is among Thailand's most important cultural and religious centers and offers among its many programs meditation courses for foreigners who wish to study the teachings of the Buddha.

No less striking than the Wat Pho reclining Buddha is the Golden Buddha that dominates the interior of Wat Trai Mit, located in the heart of Chinatown. The building isn't much to look at but deserves a visit in order to see the astonishing, enormous statue, 10 feet (3 m) high, and made of 5 tons of gold.

On the Chao Phraya's eastern bank rises the unmistakable outline of Wat Arun, the Temple of Dawn, so named because it reveals all its splendor when illuminated by the sun's first rays. Because of its enviable position, King Taksin chose it as the royal temple when the capital was moved from Ayutthaya to Thonburi. For a certain period, it even housed the Emerald Buddha. The edifice is dominated by a prang, a Khmer-style tower 260 feet (79 m) high, covered entirely with porcelain from China and encircled by four pagodas symbolizing Mount Meru, the terrestrial representation of the Buddhist paradise.

107 bottom left The yaksas that support the various
levels of the central tower, just like the main body of the
structure, are entirely decorated with ceramic fragments.

107 bottom center Facing Wat Trai Mit, famed for the
Golden Buddha worshipped there, is a more modest
bronze statue of the Enlightenment, decorated by a
garland that a worshipper has placed in homage.

107 bottom right Sometimes benevolent, sometimes
terrifying, moustache-sporting statues in the Chinese
style populate the podium of Wat Arun.

108-109 The portico surrounding Wat Arun is
bordered in part by ballast-statues with often
bizarre shapes, but also by precious Chinese
bronze statues.

110 top Episodes from the life of the Buddha are illustrated on the gleaming base of a stela in Wat Suthat.

110 bottom The arcade enclosing the wihan in Wat Suthat, the most revered in the city, holds 156 cult statues.

111 The majestic 26.5 foot (8 m) Buddha Sakyamuni in Wat Suthat was transported by river to Bangkok from Sukhothai in the distant north of Thailand in the 1800s.

112-113 A novice contemplates the setting sun in the eastern courtyard of Wat Suthat.

From the top of Wat Arun, in addition to a splendid view of the city, visitors can also see Golden Mountain, an artificial hill that King Rama III raised in the 1800s. King Rama IV completed it and had a small *chedi* built on its summit.

Later King Rama V placed in it a relic of the Buddha that had come from India. Now the golden dome of Wat Saket, a monastery famous for its precious 19th-century frescoes, caps the hill. Also to be seen are the murals from the same period that depict the Buddha's twenty-four lives. These decorate the walls of Wat Suthat, built over 27 years during the reigns of the first three sovereigns of the Chakri dynasty. The prayer room, which is called the *vihara,* is the highest in the whole city and is famous for its rich collection of precious gold images of the Buddha.

In 1846, during the reign of King Rama III, Wat Ratchanatdaram was built. Its main attraction is Loha Prasat, a dome 120 feet (36 m) high encircled by 37 spires, the only one of its kind in the country. Near this temple is located an area used for official welcoming ceremonies for heads of state and illustrious people visiting the country.

Wat Maha That, which was founded in the 18th century, is the national seat of the monastic sect Maha Nikai and incorporates the Maha That Ratchawitthayalai, one of the two Buddhist universities in the capital, which, among other programs, offer meditation courses for foreigners.

Among the temples of Bangkok, Wat Benchamabophit is one of the most "modern." It was built at the beginning of the 1900s by King Rama V, who was highly sensitive to western influences and who spared no ex-pense in its construction. The building makes extravagant use of white Carrara marble, so much so that it has earned the appellation "The Marble Temple." The windows feature stained glass from Europe. However, the splendid collection of bronzes of the Buddha kept in the interior courtyard is authentically Thai. The best time to visit the temple is in early hours of the morning, when the atmosphere is rendered especially evocative by the songs of the monks coming together to pray.

114-115 In front of the unadorned statue of a monk, a pavilion emerges on the waters of a canal near the entrance to Wat Benjamabophit.

115 top In the quiet of the temple complex, the graceful Song Phanuat in Wat Benjamabophit contains the abbot's and the monks' refectory.

115 bottom Among the many singular aspects of this wat is its unusual cladding of white Carrara marble.

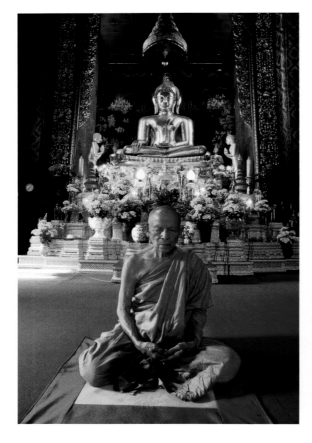

116 In the presence of the venerable statue of the Buddha, surrounded by offerings of flowers, candles and incense sticks, an elderly monk sits deep in concentration in the temple's vihara.

116-117 Monks recite morning prayers in Wat Bowon, an important temple in the center of Bangkok that dates from the mid-19th century.

118 A Hindu woman prepares to make an offering at the sanctuary of Erawan, consecrated to the Brahmin creator and his elephant Erawan.

119 top The area surrounding Erawan's chapel overflows with offerings of flowers and food. The chapel, which is located in front of the hotel, was built to propitiate deities disturbed by the heavy construction.

119 bottom left In the shadow of the sanctuary, beyond the mound of garlands left by the worshippers seeking good luck, the three impassive faces of Brahma can be glimpsed.

119 center and bottom right Incense is among the most common offerings at Erawan too, followed by crowns of flowers and yellow candles used by worshippers.

An exception among the many Buddhist temples, the Sanctuary of Erawan is dedicated to a Hindu god, Brahma, and his elephant Erawan. It is located on Ratchadamri Road and is perhaps the only temple in the world that owes its existence to a hotel. The Grand Hyatt Erawan Hotel was built next to the temple in the 1950s. Its construction seemed to be plagued by an inexplicable series of difficulties, and experts in the magic arts were called in for consultation. They established that the cause of the many problems was the dissatisfaction of the spirits disturbed by the construction. The new sanctuary was built, and the hotel was completed without further problems.

120 National flags and orange hangings with the sacred wheel, or chakra, which symbolizes Buddhism, fly in front of the large statue of the Buddha (105 ft high) that towers over the outside of Wat Indrawihan.

120-121 Nobody, even in modern Bangkok, neglects the duties of making daily offerings to the temple (in this case malai, highly perfumed flower arrangements,

and small rectangles of gold leaf) and honoring the temple's most venerated image.

121 top A young monk at Wat Indrawihan makes a traditional blessing to the kneeling worshippers. This blessing can be given upon request, or simply by entering the temple when the monk is there, and kneeling before the "altar" with the statues of Buddha.

THE PALACES OF BANGKOK

As a contrast to the redundant splendor of the reception rooms in the Royal Palace, the Vimanmek Paace, the residence that King Rama V had built at the beginning of the 1900s on the island of Ko Chang, has a more sober style and demonstrates truly regal taste.

The building's special characteristic is that it is completely made of teak, without

py period from 1902 to 1906, surrounded by all his concubines and the love of his children.

Though royal, this was a private home. It was therefore designed so that each of its 81 rooms was sheltered from indiscreet eyes, especially those of men.

Only the king's apartments could be directly reached from the outside. For the

the use of a single nail. In fact, in 1901, it was dismantled piece by piece and reassembled as it had been, but in Bangkok. The "Celestial Residence," as it is generally called, is surrounded by a long veranda that faces onto a peaceful garden dotted with reflecting lakes in which lotus flowers grow. It isn't surprising that it was the king's favorite abode, one in which he passed a long, hap-

same reason, the Throne Room, built in Italian Renaissance style (and the home of the Parliament until the 1970s), is at the entrance to the property. Inside, the period furnishings lend a special atmosphere to the spaces while objects from all over the world, including ceramics, European furniture and even a typewriter, reveal King Rama V's great enthusiasm for travel and innovation.

122 The interesting Vimanmek Palace was King Rama V's favorite residence at the beginning of the 20th century. The building is entirely made of teak, the wood traditionally used for royal residences.

122-123 The portraits exhibited at Vimanmek Palace were among the first to appear in Thailand since previously this form of art was considered a way to "steal the soul" of the subject.

Another example of the refined lifestyle that the nobility led in centuries past is the Suan Pakkad Palace, which is, in fact, a complex of six traditional wooden dwellings from various epochs and from different regions of Thailand, set in one of the most evocative gardens in Bangkok. By far the most intriguing building is the Lacquer Pavilion, whose internal walls are entirely covered with gleaming black lacquer, the result of an ancient and typically oriental technique. On these lacquered walls are magnificent gilded designs that illustrate scenes from the life of the Buddha or from the Ramayana. The pavilion, which is built on piles, comes from a place near Ayutthaya, the ancient capital, and it has recently been restored. In reality, it is complex of two temples, a library and a writing room. In the buildings, visitors can admire highly valuable objets d'art, including sculptures and ceramics. Of special importance is the Ban Chiang Pavilion where an extraordinary collection of terracotta pieces and bronze jewelry is on display. These come from the excavations supervised by Princess Chumbot around Ban Chiang, the most important Bronze Age archeological site in northeastern Thailand.

Built during the reign of King Rama V (who in the form of an equestrian statue at the entrance "greets" visitors), the Anantasamakhom displays a style of architecture that is unmistakably Italian, enhanced by the opulent frescoes that decorate its ceilings. Long used as a reception area for state ceremonies and parliamentary meetings, it is currently closed to the public. It is, however, open on one day a year, Children's Day, which is celebrated on the second Saturday in January.

The Jim Thompson Thai House Museum is, in its own way, a real palace though not a royal residence, despite having some connection to the monarchy.

Thompson "built" the house by assembling six old teak houses from the area around Ayutthaya. He then furnished it in impeccable taste, with precious antique Thai furniture, objets d'art and craft items that he had collected while traveling throughout Southeast Asia. The luxurious dwelling is a kind of ideal house in the purest Thai style, and reflects all of Thompson's taste for the beautiful and his enthusiasm for art. Though seen by some as being an American adventurer, Thompson was nonetheless responsible for reviving the Thai silk industry. He mysteriously disappeared in 1967, vanishing into thin air during a business trip in the Malaysian jungle. Was he perhaps on a secret mission? Among the thousands of suppositions about his disappearance are those that suggest the guise of businessman was only a cover for his real identity as a secret agent. However that may be, the house has remained as it was when he left it to go to Malaysia. The table is even set with silverware as if Thompson was to return at any moment.

124-125 The Lacquer Pavilion of Suan Pakkad was waken from the vicinity of Ayutthaya; it was probably decorated before the fall of the ancient capital.

124 bottom The museum-home of the mysterious Jim Thompson (businessman, spy, or both?) exemplifies the style of dwellings in Thailand's central plain.

125 Construction of the Palace of Anantasamakhom (former seat of the Parliament) was promoted by King Rama V, who was significantly more interested in the West than his predecessors.

THE MUSEUMS OF BANGKOK

Serving as both reflections and repositories of Thailand's cultural patrimony Bangkok's, numerous museums are windows that open onto a thousand-year history that expressed its complexity through the most refined art forms. Few Asian cities can boast of such rich and precious collections, often the result of the enthusiasm of cultured, enlightened sovereigns who understood not only how to preserve but also how to value the inheritance of the past in the best possible ways. It is no accident that the splendid National Museum complex dates back to 1782, the same year in which the city was founded. It is made up of a series of ancient buildings, unmistakably Thai in their architecture, situated along the Sanam Luang, which, with their collections, delineate a fascinating trip through the history of art of all of Southeast Asia. It is a trip from prehistory to the modern age that unfolds through the rooms of the two main buildings. Among numerous antiquities, visitors can admire real rarities, such as the stone stela attributed to King Ramkhamhaeng of Sukhotai, the city that, in the 13th century, became the first capital of Siam. The inscription, discov-

ered in 1833 by the future King Rama V, is considered to be the oldest in the Thai alphabet. The concepts of prosperity and piety that it expresses are still, in all senses, a cornerstone of the nation.

Also of great interest are the bronzes of Hindu deities from the Sukhotai period; the collection of filigree jewelry from the Lanna kingdom (which preceded the Siamese kingdom); stone sculptures from the Ayutthaya era that reveal clear Khmer influences; and the earliest iconographic representations of the Buddha, which come from all over Asia. In the collection, there is also the sacred and venerated statue of the Phra Sihing Buddha, second in importance only to the Emerald Buddha. The Phra Sihing Buddha is, housed in the Buddhaisawan Temple, encircled by arrays of divinities and demons depicted in fresco over two centuries ago. According to the legend, this is a figure magically created in Sri Lanka, which arrived in Sukhothai in the 13th century. Like the Emerald Buddha, this sacred image grants good fortune. For this reason, in the past, it was often the subject of contention among the cities of the north until 1795, when King Rama I brought it to the capital.

126 The National Museum houses an extraordinary collection of Buddhist works of art. In this image, the Buddha calls upon the Earth to witness his victory over the demon Mara.

127 The particularly refined features and serene expression always catch the eye in these statues of Buddha from the Sukhothai period (13th to 14th centuries).

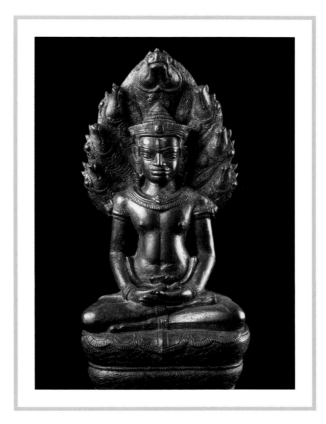

128 Elements of the face date this image of the Enlightened One to the 13th century, the Lop Buri period.

129 top Depicted in Khmer style, this Buddha in meditation is towered over by Mucilinda, the serpent that protected him from the rain.

129 bottom left The Bodhisattva Avalokitesvara extends multiple arms in this statue from the Lop Buri period.

129 bottom right King Jayavarman VII, born to the royal family of Angkor in the 12th century, brought the Khmer Empire to its greatest splendor.

Besides the buildings that house art collections, another part of the National Museum consists of some royal dwellings that show the refined lifestyle of the court in earlier times. Outstanding among these for its elegance is the Tamnak Daeng, the splendid "Red House," which was the residence of Princess Sri Sudarak, the eldest sister of Rama I. Built entirely of teak in the Ayutthaya style, it has a multi-layered sloping roof decorated with the typical swan-tail motif.

No less fascinating is the Wang Na or "Palace of the Second King," the residence of the heir nominated by the reigning sovereign, who had the privilege of taking the king's place in his absence. The interior of the Wang Na is a real treasure chest of art, overflowing with finely worked objects of gold and mother-of-pearl, in large part from the ancient capitals of Ayutthaya and Sukhothai. In addition, there is a collection of rare and unusual period instruments.

The owner of Ban Kamthieng was certainly not an aristocrat; he was instead a well-to-do farmer. His typical country home was transported piece by piece from Chiang Mai in the 1950s and reassembled near Sukhumvit Road as the part of the Siam Society's Ethnological Museum. The atmosphere of simple, frugal, mid-19th-century rural life pervades the faithfully reconstructed rooms. Furniture at that time was reduced to the minimum; some tables and mats, a large number of original utensils scattered everywhere, including agricultural tools and the characteristic nets used for fishing in the rice fields. Next to Ban Kamthieng is Sangaroon House, where visitors can see the folk craft collection assembled by the famous Thai architect Sangaroon Ratagasikorn.

130 This treasure chest of magnificent objets d'art at Wang Na, the "Palace of the Second King" has 19th-century doors decorated in gold on a black background.

130-131 Wang Na, now included in the National Museum complex, was converted into an exhibition area by Rama V in 1887.

131 bottom left Though primarily devoted to Thai art, Wang Na, also has lacquered Chinese furniture and screens.

131 bottom right Tamnak Daeng, the "Red House," owes its name to the color of the teakwood used to build the dwelling that Rama I gave to his eldest sister, Princess Sri Sudarak.

The Prasart Museum is also devoted to Thai – and more generally Asian – architecture of all styles and periods. This unusual collection of traditional houses was the goal of the rich businessman and art enthusiast, Khun Prasart. In a luxuriant park at the gates of Bangkok, a dozen or so period houses have been reconstructed. They include a royal residence inspired by the Tamnak Daeng (now part of the National Museum), a Chinese temple, a Khmer sanctuary, a library in the Sukhothai style, and a distinguished villa of European inspiration. Many of these constructions, which do not pretend to be authentic, were put together by

assembling parts of buildings from all over Asia; others were designed by Khun Prasart himself. Independent of their real or apparent age, all these buildings have been carefully designed down to the smallest details. They are splendidly decorated, with their interiors enhanced by objets d'art, Burmese sculptures, terracotta pieces and ceramics.

132-133 and 132 bottom The wood paneling of the Prasart Museum provides an interesting setting for the rare exhibits, both sacred and profane.

133 right The European-style mansion houssing the Prasart Museum recalls the somewhat hybrid pomp of royal Bangkok at the end of the 19th century.

One of the most original museums of Bangkok is surely the Royal Barge Museum which houses some of the sumptuous vessels once used by the royal court for ceremonies that took place on the Chao Praya. Until some twenty years ago, at least fifty boats took part in the annual *Kathin,* the spectacular procession on the river led by the king to celebrate the end of the rainy season. The ceremony ended with the Buddhist rite of giving new robes to the monks of Wat Arun. Built of wood over a century ago, many of the boats can no longer be safely sailed. As a result, festivities on the water have become increasingly rare. The museum, deep in the canals of Thomburi, at least allows visitors to admire the most astonishing boats at first hand. One masterpiece is the Sri *Suphanahongse,* the boat of the king and queen, with a completely decorated 165-foot (50-m) hull that ends in a fabulous gilded prow in the shape of a swan.

Scattered throughout the city are small museums devoted to more or less well known aspects of Thai culture. Among these is the Ban Chang Thai, the Marionette Museum, where visitors can see the different phases of marionette construction and occasionally attend enjoyable performances. Located on the western side of Chatuchak Park, the Hall of Railway Heritage is devoted to the typically Thai passion for railroads. It houses an exhibit of old steam locomotives and miniature trains, which complement a display on the history of railroads worldwide. On the first floor of the Metropolitan Postal Bureau, the Stamp Museum welcomes enthusiasts with its rich collection of Thai stamps and those from other countries, which visitors can simply admire or which they can purchase along with books on stamp collecting in various languages. Situated near the National Museum, the National Gallery is dedicated to modern and contemporary art. The Rare Stone Museum is an interesting exhibit of over 10,000 minerals, fossils and crystals from every part of Thailand.

The fascinating worlds of science and technology wait to astound visitors at the new museums that make up the futuristic Technopolis, citadel of knowledge and experimentation. The opening of the new Technopolis has not, however, closed the Science and Planetary Museum situated near the bus station on Sukhumvit Road. In addition to well prepared and presented scientific exhibits, especially in biology and astronomy, the museum includes among its attractions an aquarium and a planetarium. If this were not enough, a project destined to become the new Asian catalyst for the popularization of science it is going up at the gates of the city: The Science Museum, with six floors of theme-related exhibits, most of them interactive, is already open to the public. Of considerable interest is the section devoted to new technological applications in agriculture, industry, and experimental ecology in Thailand over the last decades.

134 top The Royal Barges are distinguished by having their own names and special uses.

135 A threatening kroot *sits on the cannon at the prow of one of the royal barges in the museum.*

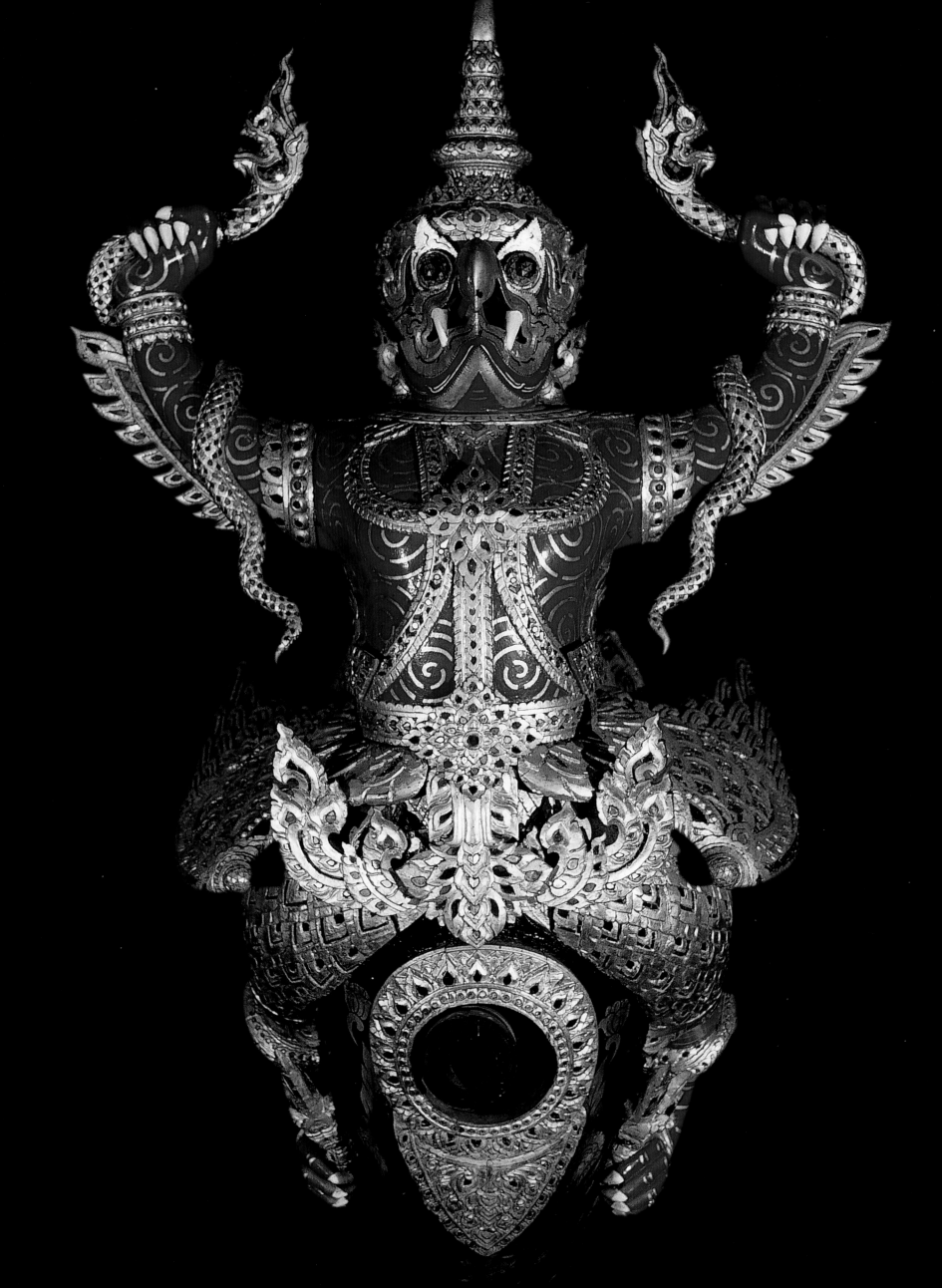

136 top left A crocodile "trainer" performs with one of the 30,000 reptiles that live on the Samut Prakan farm.

136 top right Between 6 and 11 a.m., the canals of Damnoen Saduak come alive with the country's most famous talat nam, or floating market.

136-137 At Damnoen Saduak, business is done on the water. Farmers go along the canals, exchanging products or selling them to the people living along the canal banks.

A R O U N D
B A N G K O K

There are innumerable destinations for trips to discover what lies outside Bangkok. A favorite among Thais is Samut Prakan, a place about 18 miles (30 km) from the capital. Here is the famed Muang Boran Ancient City, a sort of "Thailand in Miniature," which is certainly worth the trip. It offers a complete panorama of the architecture from every region and from several eras. Most of the 90 buildings spread throughout this open-air museum are authentic, saved *in extremis* from certain demolition.

One is the splendid library of ancient writings from Samut Songkhram. Others are faithful reconstructions or reproductions (on a reduced scale but no less interesting than the originals) of famous buildings such as the Sanphet Prasat Palace in Ayutthaya

(meticulously made by following documentation from that period) and the Grand Palace.

A team of artisans and restorers is constantly at work maintaining the complex in a perfect state, at the same time offering visitors the opportunity to admire personal demonstrations of the ancient techniques of craftsmanship that are disappearing in mod-

ern Thailand. The Crocodile Farm, also located in Samut Prakan, is an attraction of a totally different kind. Here every day at set times visitors can admire some of the more than 30,000 crocodiles raised here for their amusement.

Crocodiles, along with elephants, are the stars of the daily show put on for the pleasure of visitors to the Samohran Elephant Ground & Zoo, a type of zoo safari that extends over an area of approximately 60 acres (24 hectares) near Nakhon Pathom, about 19 miles (30 km) west of Bangkok. Here too is the Rose Garden Country Resort, a garden with a hundred varieties of roses, among which are rare and valuable ones. The resort also houses a Thai Cultural Village, which offers daily shows of traditional dances, Thai boxing, martial arts and elephant shows. For a taste of the most authentic Thai folklore, however, the visitor has to go to Damnoen Saduak, a village built on a labyrinth of canals about 50 miles (80 km) southwest of Bangkok, where every morning the most extraordinary (and most photographed) floating market in Asia opens for business.

137 top Muang Boran Ancient City, at Samut Prakan, brings together 65 buildings (both original examples and small-scale reproductions) characteristic of Thailand's distinctly different regions.

137 bottom Located in a pleasant setting of canals and bridges, some Muang Boran edifices recreate historic buildings that no longer exist.

138 and 139 An old-time atmosphere permeates
the crowded waters of Damnoen Saduak. In the 19th
century, King Rama IV had the canal which gives the
Damnoen Saduak market its name dug out; the idea
was to encourage the flow of trade, at that time
almost nonexistent in this region just south-west of
Bangkok.

140-141 Juicy, sweet tropical fruits are ready for
buying – and for eating – on the boat of a
countrywoman-trader working at Damnoen Saduak
market.

142-143 Among tidy piles of salt, a woman is absorbed in her work in a salt works at Samut Prakan, at the mouth of the Chao Praya.

143 Gathering salt in these vast flooded fields is laborious work, given the relentless sun that beats down on the Gulf of Siam. The equipment used is highly traditional: large scrapers, nets and baskets carried on the shoulders. The salt's corrosiveness makes it crucial for workers to protect their entire body.

This popular destination for day trips from Bangkok is built on an island that emerges from the Chao Phraya 43 miles (70 km) to the north of the capital. Ayutthaya can therefore also be reached by boat. Founded in 1350 by King U-Thong, it was for more than four centuries the capital of the Kingdom of Siam, acquiring at the same time the reputation of being one of the most prosperous and powerful cities in all of Indochina.

A total of thirty-three kings from various dynasties occupied Ayutthaya's throne during its period of ascendancy. But its brilliant rise was brusquely interrupted by the victory of the Burmese armies in 1767. As proof of the splendor of Ayutthaya's golden age, there are the imposing ruins of the vast Phra Nakhon Si Ayutthaya Historical Park, declared a World Heritage site by UNESCO in 1991.

The entire archeological site is dominated by the three soaring *chedis* of Wat Phra Si San Phet, the royal temple universally known as the epitome of the Ayutthaya style, the architecture of which inspired the construction of the temple of the Emerald Buddha in Bangkok. Although imposing, the temple is only a part of the immense complex that makes up the Old Palace, which, like the Grand Palace in Bangkok, was for centuries the residence of the monarchs and included places and buildings used to host official ceremonies and state visits. In the rainy season, however, they preferred to move to the summer palace in Bang Pa-In, 37 miles (60 km) north of Bangkok. This custom, begun by King Prasat Thong in 17th century, was later abandoned by the Chakri dynasty, but in the 19th century, King Chulalongkorn rediscovered its quiet fascination. He devoted himself to the construction of a fabulous royal summer palace, an elegant complex of buildings in Thai, Chinese and European styles surrounded by a lake and shaded by laburnum.

144 top left and 145 Nine restored prangs stand in Wat Chai Wattanaram, built in the 1600s to celebrate a victory over Cambodia.

144 top right Built to contain the ashes of three sovereigns, the chedis of Wat Phra Si Sanpet were built in the largest temple complex of Ayutthaya, the ancient capital.

144 bottom left This serene visage of the Buddha, embraced by the roots of a ficus religiosa tree conveys Ayutthaya's somewhat melancholy atmosphere.

144 bottom right The prang of Wat Phra Ram, one of the most imposing in Ayutthaya, was built at the end of the 4th century and restored a century later.

146 top left and center The restored arcade surrounding the prang, Wat Putthaisawan, contains interesting gilded statues of the Buddha.

146 top right A resplendent modern chedi stands in Wat Suan Luang, in the area once occupied by the royal palace.

146-147 Three students pray in front of the reclining Buddha at Wat Yai Chai Mongkol, a large temple erected in 1593 to celebrate a victory over the Burmese.

147 top A row of Buddhas lined up in Wat Yai Chai Mongrol. The temple, outside Ayutthaya, was built in the 14th century as a place for meditation.

147 bottom Facing the abbot, who leads the prayers, a group of monks assembles at the feet of the Buddha in the Bot of Wat Yai Chai Mongkol.

Fewer than 50 miles (30 km) separate Bangkok from the Gulf of Thailand with its dazzling beaches; among these shines the star of Pattaya, a resort that became popular during the Vietnam War. The U.S. marines stationed at the American base at Nakhon Ratchasima used to spend their leave in this fishing village set on a perfect crescent of white sand. Today, it is a fashionable holiday destination, offering sports and all kinds of beach activities by day and a wild nightlife after dusk; this latter centers on the Strip on the south side of Pattaya Beach, thronged with crowded open-air bars, discos and restaurants.

Half way between Bangkok and Pattaya is the quiet coastal town of Chonburi. Here the main activity is oyster cultivation, and visitors come to admire the giant statue of the Buddha in the Wat Dhama Nimitr monastery and to see the precious 18th-century frescoes in the Wat Yai Intharam, both of which are pilgrimage sites for Thais.

150 top Only a small fishing village thirty years ago, Pattaya is now a bustling resort complete with imposing hotels.

150 bottom Situated on the Gulf of Thailand, southwest of the capital, vibrant Pattaya is a completely modern city.

151 top Renowned for its "dubious" offerings, Tiffany's Show is one of Pattaya's most famous nightspots and perfectly embodies its worldly spirit.

151 bottom The Pattaya area includes three bays: Pattaya Beach, 2.5 miles (4 km) long; Jomtien Beach, a windsurfer's paradise; and Naklua Bay, the quietest of the three.

For completely different reasons, Kanchanaburi, a small town on the banks of the River Kwai, at edge of the western forests, has entered literary and film history. It is the site of the famous "Bridge over the River Kwai."

During World War II, the Japanese used over 60,000 prisoners to build the bridge and rail line that was intended to link Thailand with Burma.

The key element of the project was the bridge, destroyed by American bombers in 1945 but later immortalized in Pierre Boulle's bestseller *The Bridge over the River Kwai* and in David Lean's film of the same name.

Both powerfully recall the sacrifice of over 8000 men who died during construction and who are buried in the city's two cemeteries.

152-153 The famous "Bridge over the River Kwai" at Kanchanaburi was completed in 1943 at the cost of thousands of human lives. In 1945 it sustained damage from Allied bombers, but was repaired after the war.

153 top "Long-tail boats" for visitors are moored by the floating restaurants set up on River Kwai's east bank, next to the bridge.

153 bottom left Construction of the Thailand-Burma railway is estimated to have cost the lives of 112,000 prisoners of war. An 50-miles (80-km) stretch is still intact.

153 bottom right In Kanchanaburi War Cemetery some 7000 gravestones form silentrows. The epitaph, almost always the same, is brief and haunting: "A man who died for his country."

154-155, 155 top and bottom Demarcating the Thailand-Laos border for 465 miles (750 km), the River Mekong finally flows more calmly after a tumultuous course.

155 center The Mekong abounds in fish and is a source of food for the local people. Thanks to the progressive opening up of Laos, the river is no longer a barrier but a point of contact between the two countries.

156 top *Founded in the 13th century as capital of the Lanna kingdom, Chiang Mai, the "New City," still retains parts of its ancient city wall intact.*

156-157 *Chinese New Year fills Chiang Mai's streets of with colors and sounds. The celebration, based on the lunar calendar, falls between January and February.*

157 top left and right *For the Chiang Mai's Chinese community, New Year is the most important festival, and they celebrate it for three consecutive days.*

157 bottom left *Thanks to rapid development in recent years, bustling Chiang Mai is northern Thailand's biggest city, with 250,000 inhabitants.*

157 bottom right *At the foot of an interesting modern chedi, a pedal-powered rickshaw prepares to enter modern Chiang Mai, east of the old town.*

THE NORTH AND THE "GOLDEN TRIANGLE"

In Thailand, the words "the North" can only mean "the Golden Triangle," an imprecise but evocative geographical name that originally denoted the exact point on the River Mekong where the borders of Burma, Laos and Thailand came together. The borders of the Golden Triangle then expanded to include the large, legendary region of the opium plantations once operated by the Kuomintang. More prosaically, the vast north is still a wild region, and its fascination is enriched by the presence of remote valleys inhabited by tribes from afar, forgotten cities which played a fundamental role in the country's history, and impenetrable forests where real adventure is still possible. But visitors shouldn't expect to come face to face with smugglers and traffickers; and as for the opium plantations – if they still exist, after the Thai government's repeated attempts to quash drug production

and trafficking – they're practically inaccessible. Visitors venturing into the far north will find excitement of a very different kind, but no less intense; like the thrill of a trip on a pirogue on the Mekong at sunset, when the majestic river's waters turn red.

158-159 This statue of the Buddha, housed in an elaborate frame that imitates the shape of a sanctuary, is kept in Wat Phra Singh in Chiang Mai.

159 top At the end of the 14th century, the king of Chiang Mai had the large chedi of Wat Suan Dok built to house a miraculous relic from Sri Lanka.

159 top center A monk reads in the quiet meeting room of Wat Phra Singh, the most important temple in Chiang Mai's urban area.

159 bottom center Wat Phra Singh was built in 1345 with two aims: to hold the ashes of King Kham Fu and to become the religious center of the Lanna kingdom.

159 bottom Many different representations of the Buddha surround a young monk at Wat Phra Singh.

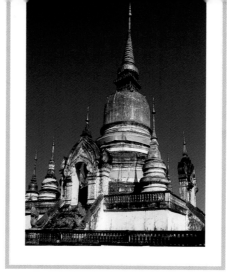

Or an encounter with the Burmese who cross the border every day to make purchases at the Mae Sai market, where among all kinds of goods on sale, delightful Burmese handicraft work can be found. The main city of northern Thailand is Chiang Mai, which, ever since it was founded in 1296 as capital of Lanna Thai, Thailand's first independent kingdom, has always been the religious, cultural and commercial center of the north. Thailand's second largest city is situated about 435 miles (700 km) north of Bangkok, and thus remained isolated from the rest of the country for a long time; this meant it was able to maintain its own cultural identity, and its many temples accentuate the old capital's proud character. Indeed, the city's most famous monument is a temple, the Wat Phrathat Doi Suthep. It stands on the top of Mount Doi Suthep and can only be reached by climbing up a stairway of over 300 steps flanked by sculptures of the seven-headed *nagas* (the snakes of eastern mythology). But it's worth the climb: the temple is truly extraordinary with its incredible gold-covered *chedi*, which offers a spectacular panorama over the city and the valley.

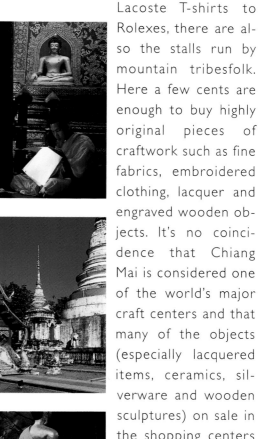

Chiang Mai's other great feature is the Chang Klan Road Market, better known as the Night Market, as it is held each night from 6.00 to 11.00. This is a true shopper's paradise, and as well as the sea of stalls selling all kinds of fake designer goods from Lacoste T-shirts to Rolexes, there are also the stalls run by mountain tribesfolk. Here a few cents are enough to buy highly original pieces of craftwork such as fine fabrics, embroidered clothing, lacquer and engraved wooden objects. It's no coincidence that Chiang Mai is considered one of the world's major craft centers and that many of the objects (especially lacquered items, ceramics, silverware and wooden sculptures) on sale in the shopping centers in Bangkok and other major visitors' resorts come from the city's workshops.

The artisans of Bor Sang ("Parasol Village") specialize in making typical rice paper umbrellas decorated with traditional designs, and the village of San Kamphaeng is famous for its fine silks. Chiang Mai is a very good base for day trips to the villages of the nomadic tribes of Chinese, Burmese and Tibetan origin, which live in scattered communities in the hills rising above the valley.

160-161 Little chedi built in memory of deceased prominent and religious figures rise above the sacred images of Wat Jet Yot, outside the perimeter of the old city.

161 top The very unusual structure of the chedi of Wat Jet Yot (several spires dominate it) has given the complex its name: the "Monastery of the Seven Spires."

161 center left Another unusual chedi rises over Wat Phuak Hong: built in 1517, the 7-story structure has 58 niches.

161 center right The plaster figures adorning the base of Wat Jet Yot have miraculously survived the ravages of time and the Burmese, they depict divinities in yoga positions.

161 bottom left Lanna architecture, seen here in a detail of the vihara of Wat Phuak Hong, typically features refined carving in golden wood.

161 bottom right A guard of the vihara of Wat Phuak Hong below a "hook" typical of temple roofs. The cho fa is a stylized rendering of a heavenly creature.

162 and 163 A few miles south of Chiang Mai stand the great pink stone chedi of Wat Chedi Liam and the buildings of the complex. These are decorated with golden carvings typical of Lanna architecture and guarded by images of monstrous figures. Built in 1286, this is the most interesting temple complex of Wiang Kum Kam, a pretty town which is probably much older than the capital itself and which boasts over 20 sites with temple ruins.

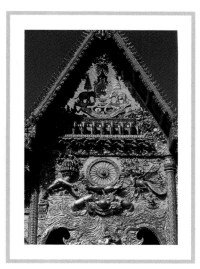

164 Wat Hua Khuang, a fairly small temple, is very interesting, as is the remote town which is its home: Nan, east of Chiang Mai.

165 top right A complex carved decoration in the northern style surrounds the chakra, the "wheel,"a symbol of the future and royalty, on the façade of Wat Hua Khuang.

165 center left The graceful chedi of Wat Phaya Wat in Nan combines local artistic influences with those of Lanna and Lan Chang.

165 center right A frieze of elephants (for good fortune) decorates a column in Wat Phumin, the town of Nan's most interesting temple complex.

165 bottom left and right The carvings of Wat Phumin show influences from nearby Laos, as does the statue of the Buddha in the bot.

166 and 167 *The paintings in Wat Phumin were done by unknown artists in the 19th century; they show a great variety of subject matter, from religious themes to legends, and also present scenes of everyday life.*

Another particularly popular trip is an excursion in a pirogue along the River Kok, up to Chiang Rai. Situated in a green valley in the heart of the Golden Triangle, and surrounded by the Akha tribe's villages, Chiang Rai was founded in the 13th century and for a long time was the capital of the Lanna kingdom. That period, the most glorious in the kingdom's history, was when a number of temples were built, including Wat Ngam Muang, which holds the remains of King Mengrai, founder of the city, and Wat Phra That Doi Tung, which dominates the town from the top of a mountain.

Lampang is a lively provincial town,

known for its Burmese-style temples such as the magnificent Wat Lampang Luang, which dates back to the 15th century. Above all, the town is famous for the Thai Elephant Conservation Center, dedicated to protecting the animal (Thailand's national symbol) and the ancient local traditions that involved it. The Center is a large park open to the public; it includes an elephant training ground where visitors can watch the pachyderms in a daily show and can go on short trips into the forest riding on the back of an elephant.

170 and 171 Lampang, south east of Chiang Mai, boasts a Lanna monastery complex: Wat Lampang Luang, which was originally a fortress in the 11th century.

172 and 173 Five centuries of exposure to the elements have left their mark on the rich decorations of Vihara Nam Tam, considered to be the oldest wooden building in Thailand.

174 and 175 Wat Lampang Luang has valuable Lanna statues with a design element found only in the North: the ku, in golden brick, which holds the main image.

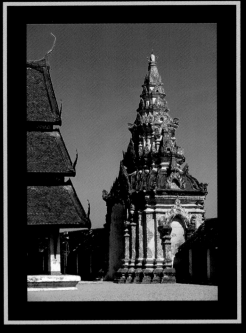

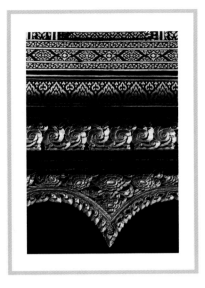

176 top and bottom left Naturalistic and symbolic friezes decorate Wat Haripunchai, in Lamphun, founded in the 9th century to house a chapel of the Enlightened One.

176 center left This niche in the chedi at Wat Kukut, in Lamphun (from 1218) contains statues showing various mudra, or symbolic hand gestures

176 bottom right Elaborate flaming cho fa and extremely stylised naga serpents adorn the sloping roofs of buildings at Wat Harinpunchaia

177 With its 50 m height, the spire of the Sri Lankan-style chedi at Wat Haripunchaia (from 1443) dominates a crowd of monks and novices.

178 top A snow-white mosque, more commonly seen in the south than in the north of the country, stands out on the outskirts of Mae Salong, where Muslims of Burmese origin live.

178 center Farmers from the Mae Salong area sell their vegetables outside the wall which separates a wat from the town center's streets.

178 bottom Mahouts, dressed in their typical blue cassocks and vegetable-fiber helmets, guide three elephants from the Elephant Training Center across a river near Chiang Dao.

178-179 The pagoda of the Princess Mother, built in modern times, rises impressively above the rolling hills near Mae Salong, the city which it now symbolizes.

Hidden in a valley surrounded by imposing mountains, on the border with Burma, Mae Hong Son is the smallest and most isolated of the northern provinces. It can be reached only by plane or a 10-hour car journey along the only road that goes up northwest of Chiang Mai, climbing up over the first spurs of the Himalayas. The relative inaccessibility of this remote area of the country has

mosphere where rampant nature rules supreme and conquers visitors with the enticing call to adventure. It is no coincidence that this region is known as Shangri-La, "the Land of Happiness."

The mountain tribes' villages are dotted throughout the teak forests, and can be reached by trekking, often using the smugglers' tracks.

preserved it – at least until recently – from the onslaught of tourism. Mae Hong Son is little more than a village, and does not actually have much to offer apart from a couple of temples in the Burmese style. However, the valley makes up for it as it is astonishingly beautiful, immersed in a wild-west type at-

180 top and bottom left The province of Mae Hong Son, practically isolated until the 1970s, is mainly dedicated to agriculture.

180 top right As it is near the first spurs of the Himalayas, the land around Mae Hong Son often has abundant rainfall which feeds the rivers and waterfalls.

180 bottom right Rice nears readiness for harvesting at the end of the rainy season, between November and March.

180-181 A thin veil of fog often enhances the attractiveness of the tranquil rural landscapes of the Northwest.

182-183 Irrigated areas often turn into huge "archipelagoes" on which the peasants work with the help of small boats to move heavy loads.

182 bottom left and 183 right The land is usually worked without the use of agricultural machinery. The few tractors available are normally used to do work traditionally once done with oxen and buffaloes.

182 bottom right A chao na, "rice grower," winnows the harvest from the fields by beating it on a wooden chute. The net stops the precious grains from getting lost.

This is true jungle in every sense of the word; the best idea for the adventurous visitor is to hire a local guide who not only knows the places and tribal dialects but will also make you feel you are in safe hands. With such a guide, it is possible to venture into Karen territory, where the legendary "giraffe women" live, take a pirogue and battle the rapids of the Pai river up to the Burmese border, and then continue with long hikes in the forest.

This way visitors can seek out the villages of the Lahu, the nomads who came from China, and the Lisu, who came from Tibet, and who can be identified by their colorful traditional costumes.

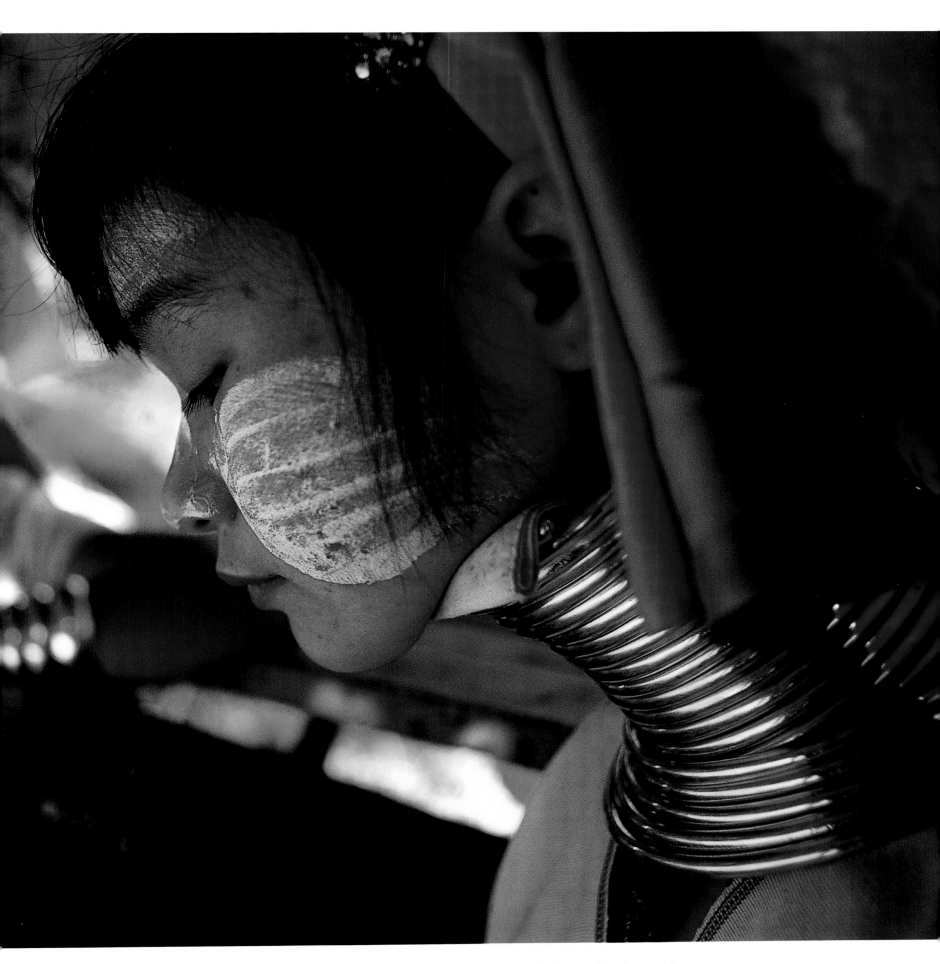

186 top The Padaung from the Burmese province of Kayah who have settled in Thailand generally live in the adjacent region of Mae Hong Son.

186 center top Eesthetic reasons and indication of social status are behind the customary neck elongation Padaung "giraffe women."

186 center bottom This little girl probably won't wear rings around her neck; indeed, Padaung mothers are increasingly less willing to force this tradition on their daughters.

186 bottom Apart from the "rational" explanation for the custom, it is said that the rings saved the "giraffe women" from slavery (it was impossible to sell them) or from tigers.

186-187 The first ring is worn at about 6 years of age. By the time a Padaung woman reaches the marrying age, her neck may be up to 10 inches (25 cm) longer than normal.

Phitsanulok is a must-see along the classic itinerary between Bangkok and the north of the country. It had its moment of glory during the Ayutthaya period when, among many other monuments, Wat Phra Si Rattana Mahathat was built, where worshippers pray to the Phra Buddha Chinaraj, a precious holy statue from 1357 which is considered one of the most beautiful in the whole of Thailand. Set in a valley protected by gently rolling hills, about 217 miles (350 km) south of Chiang Mai, is Sukhothai.

188 top Phra Buddha Chinaraj, at Wat Mahathat in Phitsanulok, is considered second in importance only to the Emerald Buddha of Wat Phra Kaeo.

188-189 Incense sticks and votive candles carry the hopes of worshippers in the perfumed air of Wat Mahathat, also known as Wat Yai, "big temple."

189 top left A potent sacred image, amongst the most venerated in Thailand, Phra Buddha Chinaraj was forged in bronze at the end of the Sukhothai era, in the 14th century.

189 top right In a solemn atmosphere an official ceremony with flower and food offerings (fruit and a pig's head) takes place at Wat Phra Si Ratana.

189 bottom left Numerous yellow candles burn as a sign of homage in Wat Mahathat, the "Great Chedi of the Relic" in Phitsanulok.

189 bottom right Behind the Buddha depicted in the mudra of "preventing calamities," rises the 14th-century prang of Wat Mahathat, in the Ayutthaya style.

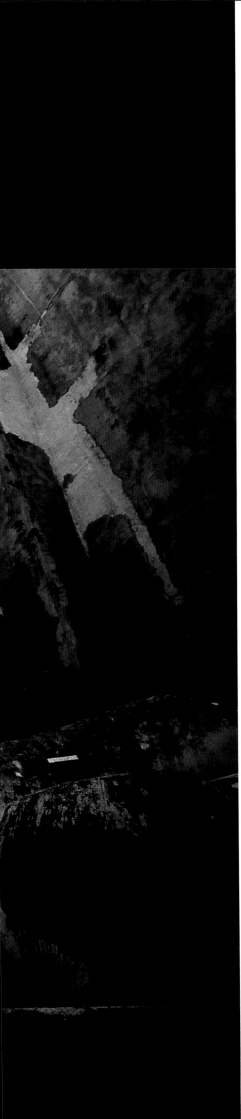

This was Siam's earliest capital and the elegance of its artistic forms bears witness to the power of a kingdom as enlightened as it was ancient, that dated back to the 12th century and was the birthplace of the Thai nation. Wrapped in a magical aura, the Historical Park of Sukhothai is one of the most interesting archeological areas of the country. The ruins of the temples stand proud among tidy lawns and lotus-flower lakes, in a timeless atmosphere. The Ramkhamhaeng National Museum holds a vast collection of Sukhothai-period artifacts found in the area, and provides a valuable historical introduction to the Sukhothai era. But it is the monuments that are most enchanting, with the grandeur of Wat Mahathat, the most important temple, and the transcendental serenity of the enormous sitting Buddha, 50 feet (50 m) tall.

190 top A row of monks or bodhisattya – enlightened figures who are more or less equivalent to Christian saints – pay respect to the Buddha in a frieze at Wat Mahathat in Sukhothai.

190-191 The largest surviving sacred statue of Sukhothai, in Wat Si Chum, is 50 feet (15 m) high; its hands and legs are covered in sheets of gold leaf applied by worshippers.

191 top left A large modern statue imitates the graceful forms of the Sukhothai style.

191 top right The Wat Mahathat complex was enlarged in several phases; by the 16th century it included 200 chedi.

191 bottom left and bottom right The "lotus bud" summit of Wat Mahathat's central chedi towers over one of the smaller towers that surround the heart of the complex.

191 center right Two rows of columns that flank the seated statue of the Buddha are all that remains of the ancient vihara of Wat Mahathat.

*192 top left Wat Sa Si has a chedi inspired by the shape
of the Sri Lankan stupa.*

*192 top right The squat prang of Wat Si Sawai were
probably part of a Khmer complex.*

*192 bottom A worshipper ties a ribbon around the trunk of
one of the 24 elephants that hold up the chedi at Wat
Sarasak.*

*193 Worn-away columns flank the great Buddha at Wat
Saphan Hin, at the western end of Sukhothai.*

Around 44 miles (70 km) away stands Si Satchanalai, the twin-town of Sukhothai dedicated to Buddha, which is just as splendid although smaller and less imposing. The temples, which date from the 13th century, are scattered over the hills, in a wild, highly evocative landscape.

194 top left The magnificent Wat Mahathat in Si Satchanalai, built during the Khmer era, was turned into a Buddhist temple during the Sukhothai period.

194 bottom left A section of a frieze that can be seen at Wat Mahathat in Si Satchanalai, the biggest satellite town of the capital Sukhothai, 31 miles (50 km) to the west.

194-195 A chedi in Sri Lankan style stands over Si Satchanalai: the site, which is marked by an imposing architectural style, was heavily fortified.

196 top Tourist development in the Hua Hin area, on the east coast of the Kra Isthmus, began almost a century ago.

196-197 These fishing-boats recall Hua Hin's origins. The only traces of its fishing-village past are found near the jetty.

197 top left An old-style locomotive is kept in the interesting station at Hua Hin, a stop-off point of the Eastern & Oriental Express.

197 top right Modern beach facilities at Hua Hin, where tourism is once again as popular as it was in the early 20th century.

197 bottom left Hua Hin is not just towering hotels: as the king's favorite holiday spot c. 1900, it was soon enriched by the villas of Thai society.

197 bottom right In the evening, the busy Chatchai market in Hua Hin offers the best of the daily haul.

THE SOUTH AND THE ISLANDS

Magnificent palm-fringed beaches, coral reefs, gorgeous tropical islands, lush forests, extraordinarily beautiful marine parks, quiet fishing villages and historical cities: the south of Thailand is all this, and much more. It is no surprise, then, that this region of Thailand is among international tourism's best-loved destinations. Geographically, it lies along the Kra Isthmus, which stretches from Chumphon to the border with Malaysia, 620 miles (1000 km)

south of Bangkok, lapped on the west by the Indian Ocean and on the east by the warm waters of the Gulf of Thailand. Just where the Gulf starts to widen is Hua Hin, the country's oldest seaside resort. In 1910 Prince Chakrabongse, on a hunting expedition in the jungle, by chance came across a magnificent beach and was so taken with it that he decided to build his summer resi-

dence there. The royal palace was soon surrounded by the luxurious villas of courtiers and Bangkok high society, and even today this area is considered a sort of Riviera, where the Thais who count come on holiday. But most of all, it is the retreat of the royal family, which baptized its summer palace "Klai Kangwon" ("Far from Worries"). The city has kept a pleasant colonial atmosphere which is accentuated by the old villas, tastefully restored colonial-style hotels and the old railway station in the Thai style,

which is truly picturesque with its royal waiting room. Cha Am is about 12 miles (20 km) away from Hua Hin, but together the two resorts for a practically unbroken stretch of tourist developments. Unlike its sophisticated neighbor, Cha Am is a calm, relaxed seaside resort, enhanced by its lovely beach, on which luxurious international-class hotels are being built.

At the opposite end of the Kra Isthmus, in Thailand's far south, is Songkhla, a quiet frontier town inhabited by Malaysian, Thais and Chinese. It stands on a strip of land between the sea and Thale Luang Kake, which is some 62 miles (80 km) long, an extraordinary oasis of nature, home to hundreds of bird species. It is certainly hard to imagine that this idyllic place used to be the stronghold of the pirates who raged along the coasts of Malaysia and the Gulf of Siam, in which at least eight islands are scattered. The largest is Koh Samui, edged with powdery white beaches said to project an extremely positive aura. Or at least that is what the new-age philosophers believe; they were among the first to discover this simple and charming island and made it one of the Asian hotspots for regeneration of mind and body. In recent years, several centers for meditation, alternative medicine, and holistic activities have sprung up on the beaches and in the shade of the palm trees, transforming the island into a kind of "fountain of eternal youth." The best way for the visitors to get around the island is to hire a moped; using it they can discover secret bays and fishing villages or explore the coconut palm plantations inland. One 62-mile (80-km) main road circles the whole island, offering glimpses of breathtaking panoramas along some stretches. Visitors leaving Na Thon (the city that has developed around the port) and traveling clockwise can stop off at Bo Phut Bay village, visit the monastery of the Great Buddha and then continue on to Chaweng and Lamai, the fashionable beaches on the island's east coast. This is a developed area, full of hotels, luxury restaurants, and open-air bars.

198 top left Of panoramic interest rather than cultural value, the Great Buddha dominates Bo Phut, on Ko Samui.

198 top right Na Thon, the capital of Ko Samui, is the landing point for anyone arriving from the mainland.

198-199 The modern temple Nuam Naram, on Ko Samui, rises above a crown of artificial flowers.

199 top A traditional-style kiosk stands opposite a cottage at Chaweng Beach.

199 center and bottom Ban Bophut has kept the timeless appeal of a traditional fishing village.

Along with Ko Samui, Ko Pha Ngan and Ko Tao are the only inhabited islands in the Samui archipelago; they offer truly unspoiled areas and panoramas which won't disappoint those who dream of an ecological albeit Spartan holiday.

visitors' accommodations confirm this impression; they are simple yet welcoming with their bungalows on the shores of dream beaches, silent and secluded, from where visitors can set off on unforgettable underwater adventures. The most popular

On Ko Pha Ngan, for a start, there are no tarmac roads (at least not yet), and on arrival the visitor has the distinct sensation of having arrived in heaven on earth. The

beach is that at Hat Rin, which is invaded at every full moon by the bacchanals of the Full Moon Party, the wildest party in Thailand.

200 top The rivulets of the southernmost of the two waterfalls at Namuang, inland on Ko Samui, feed a natural pool of pleasantly lukewarm water.

200 center left The mosque of Ko Panyi, in the bay of Phang Nga, stands among the pile-dwellings of the Muslim village

200 center right Visiting monks arrive at Ko Panyi. Muslims and Buddhist live in harmony all over Thailand.

200 bottom left Run aground on the coast of Ko Samui, this medium-size fishing boat will be able to go to sea in the evening, when the high tide comes in.

200 bottom right A fruit-and-drinks seller walks along one of the dazzling white sand beaches that have made Ko Samui's fortune.

200-201 Slender coconut palms overhang a solitary bay on Ko Samui. Outside the villages, beyond the first layer of vegetation, the forest is impenetrable.

Beautiful Krabi is set on the Indian Ocean, and is an upcoming location on the Thai tourism scene. Until a few decades ago, Krabi was just a fishing village that awoke each day to the chatter of the morning market, and then dozed off again, completely unaware of its treasure trove of heavenly beaches. The beaches were not yet named on the maps but their reputation was spread by word of mouth among globetrotters. They had found a true earthly paradise on the Kra Isthmus, with simple straw-and-

bamboo hotels where they could sleep and eat their fill of fish, spending next to nothing in the process. This enchantment seemed destined to end when an American glossy magazine proclaimed Ao Phra Nang beach – a tropical beach of fine pink sand that stands out against the limestone cliffs – to be one of the most beautiful in the world.

202 top left The outlines of a fish-farm's "cages." Fish-farming is fast-developing industry in Thailand.

202 top right Lines of coconut palms border the coast road in the bay of Phang Nga.

202-203, 203 top and bottom Krabi town sits along the estuary of the Krabi river. Fishermen use either long-tail boats or fishing-boats. They haul in large amounts of fish and seafood, either from fish farms or caught in nets.

Since then Krabi has literally "exploded," but without totally destroying its attractive nature. New resorts have been built; they are among the most luxurious in the country. However, construction has been done with minimum environmental impact by camouflaging Thai-style bungalows and pavilions in the jungle and even avoiding building roads in the Cape Phra Nang area, which can be reached only by sea. These precautions help safeguard the area's wild beauty.

Located here is the legendary Princess Cave, a place that is said to have magical powers, not least the protection of fisherman who venture out to sea. Not far from there is the monastery of the Tiger Cave, an extremely mystical place deep in the woods, where the monks worship a footprint of the Buddha set into the rock.

Hundreds of rocks, islands and tree-covered pinnacles scattered over an area of over 80 sq. miles (200 sq. km) make up Phang Nga Bay, the most extraordinary Thai marine park, which separates the coast of Krabi from the island of Phuket. The largest islands conceal salt lakes inland, which can only be reached through the caves cut into the rock-face but which are often hidden by the high tide. Because of this, the most interesting and ecological way of exploring this unspoiled paradise is to use inflatable canoes.

Gliding through the darkness of the passages you come out in the inland lakes where nature presents an awe-inspiring, primordial spectacle: the steep sides are covered in jungle and mangroves, the glassy water is an incredible emerald hue, while fishing falcons circle above.

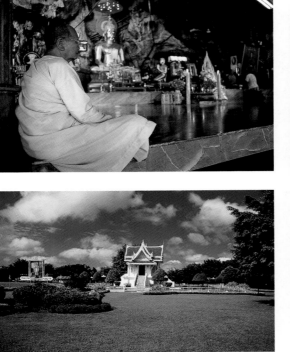

204-205 A monk lights votive candles before a corpulent fo tuo, *a Chinese-style Buddha, in Wat Tham Seua.*

205 top Wat Tham Seua is an unusual temple, situated in a low natural cave, the wall of which can be made out behind the Buddha.

205 center left and bottom right A nun meditates next to the golden statue of the Buddha in the wat. (right) The temple has about 250 monks and nuns.

205 bottom left In an airy garden in Krabi stands the "pillar of the city," a remnant of an ancient tradition. The pillar said to hold the city's protective spirits.

206-207 and 207 top In the bay of Phang Nga, fishing is the most exploited natural resource: together with the province of Krabi, the area has 248 fishing villages.

207 center and bottom The unusual-shaped peaks of the bay of Phang Nga were created 130 million years ago by the thrusting up of an ancient coral reef.

Phuket Island, linked to mainland Thailand by the Sarasin bridge, is shaped like a round pearl and has earned the name "Pearl of the Andaman Sea," by which it is known throughout the world. The island's surface area is about 220 sq. miles (570 sq. km), mostly taken up by a mountain range that culminates in the 1750 foot (529 m) high peak of Mai Tha Sip Song. The rest of the land is level and used for the traditional cul-

came from tin, which abounded in the local mines and used to be considered almost as precious as gold was in ancient times. As a result, business flourished on the island's coasts and for centuries it was an important port of call along the merchant route between India and China and enjoyed a long period of prosperity. Its bays provided safe anchorage for passing ships; they could take cover from the fury of the monsoons or

tivation of rice, coconut palms, pineapples and rubber trees, the basis of the local economy. In the last few decades international tourism has given this economy a considerable boost has made Phuket, Thailand's largest island, one of the world's most popular and famous vacation destinations.

However, in the past, the island's wealth

wait for favorable winds to enable them to continue crossing the Andaman Sea. Those same bays and inlets, hemmed with white sandy beaches shaded by palm trees, today have an irresistible appeal for tourists. Patong beach, a strip of powdery sand some 2.4 miles (4 km) long, is one of the most beautiful but also the most crowded and an-

208-209 Studded with yachts, the bay of Nai Harn opens up on the southern tip of Phuket Island, facing the Andaman Sea.

209 top and bottom left Hat Patong, Phuket's most famous beach, has developed — upward as well as outward — and shows no sign of stopping.

209 top right Over the years, Phuket has knocked Pattaya off its pedestal as a tourist center: Phuket's beaches, which go on for miles, are considered among the best in the world.

209 bottom right Maps of Phuket usually only show one main center, Phuket Town (Muang Phuket in Thai), but in fact the island's beach resorts are growing.

imated: a bathing spot by day and a nightlife hotspot after sunset.

But vacationers only have to go to the south of the island, where the most spellbinding beaches are clustered, to discover glorious bays and inlets.

These are not exactly secluded and certainly have a busy focal point: Nai Harn Beach is the home of the Phuket Yacht Club

and there is the Samnak Song Nai Han, a monastic center situated right on the seashore. A charming atmosphere envelops Surin beach, north of Patong, where the most luxurious resorts are situated; given its perfect west-facing position, it is considered one of the best places from which to admire Phuket's fiery sunsets.

The chief town of the island is Phuket Town, with a population of around 60,000. It was founded at the end of the 19th century by Chinese and Malaysian merchants who had gone there to exploit the numerous tin mines, and it still has a multi-ethnic feel to it. That flourishing era of business and commerce is evoked by the Sino-Portuguese style houses that make up the colonial quarter; its sumptuous buildings meld Chinese and European architectural elements.

210 top and bottom Marvelous Karon Beach, on the west coast of Phuket, is generally quieter than Patong, which is just further north.

210-211 Phuket's six golf clubs offer excellent courses, which are much appreciated by Thais: this sport is popular all over the country.

211 top and right Kata Beach, Karon and Nai Harn, all on the west coast of the island, follow one upon another a range of 6 miles (10 km) as the crow flies.

Perfect examples are the splendid Provincial Court, which has retained the original wooden judge's bench and is still used as a courthouse today, and Provincial Hall, the seat of several public offices, which is famous for its 99 doors. Just outside the city is Wat Chalong, the largest of the 29 Buddhist monasteries on the island; here the 18th-century monk Luang Pho Chaem is worshipped – he was an expert in traditional medicine and a renowned orthopedic doctor. The Thais hold the blessing of this monastery's monks in high esteem; they make pilgrimages there to obtain the holy ribbon that, if worn tied around the wrist, is believed to be an incredible good-luck charm with the power to prevent accidents and illness.

212-213 A statue of an elephant opposite a wat in Phuket Town receives offerings from worshippers: in Thailand elephants (chang) are considered to be sacred.

212 bottom On the central thanon in Phuket Town are gracious colonial-style villas, built at the turn of the 19th century by Chinese merchants who had settled on the island.

213 top Phuket Town, which is less "artificial" than the beach resorts on the island, has a Thai-style market and a typical night market which opens after dusk.

213 bottom In Phuket Town's modern streets, a number of corners have been embellished by street furniture such as pretty circular fountains.

214 top and 215 top right Wat Khajorn, at Phuket Town, boasts numerous classical chedi, clad in brightly colored tiles.

214 center Wat Chalong is considered to be the most important temple on Phuket Island. In the 19th century, two of its abbots were famous herbalists and healers.

214 bottom There are several statues of the Buddha in the main hall of Wat Chalong, where the local people often come to obtain predictions about the future.

215 top left The classically proportioned vihara of Wat Mongkol Nimit, in Phuket Town, dominates one of the island's 29 monastic complexes.

214-215 On high ground near the old village of Thalang, north of Phuket Town, one can admire a large reclining Buddha, the largest statue on the island.

Not only is Phuket a first-class vacation destination but it also makes an excellent base for exploring the Thai archipelagoes. First, the Phi Phi Islands, which are by far the most beautiful of the Andaman Sea. They form a stunning coral archipelago with a fragile ecosystem that was saved from the effects of tourism some years ago when fortunately it was made into a National Marine Park. Phi Phi Don, the bigger of the two islands, rises magnificently with its peaks covered in vegetation and its emerald waters, concealing fabulous beaches among the

rocks. In fact it is not one, but two islands, linked by a palm-covered strip of sand that forms enchanting twin bays, with shallow water and a seabed thick with coral and tropical fish. Smaller and less known, Phi Phi Le is completely uninhabited and has no tourist facilities. But it is certainly worth visiting in a traditional pirogue to discover wonderful little hidden beaches, make a trip to Pilay Lake, set like a jewel among the mountains, or visit the imposing Viking Cave. Ths cave, hidden between steep cliffs, is a refuge for a myriad of swallows; it is also where the chao lay, the mysterious sea gypsies, climb up on vertiginous bamboo scaffolding to perform their balancing acts while collecting swallows' nests. These are considered a delicacy and are then sold for their weight in gold to Chinese restaurants in Phuket.

216 left Under the well-placed shade of the palm trees, bungalows with traditional style roofs look onto the sea of Ko Phi Phi Don.

216-217 Colored good-luck ribbons hang from the bows of "long-tail" boats moored on the beach at Ao Ton Sai.

217 right Having left the landing stage of Ao Ton Sai, a hired boat is an ideal way to discover the treasures of Ko Phi Phi Don, one of the most famous tropical islands in the world.

THE NORTHEAST
(THE I-SAN)

Thailand's endless northeastern plain, which extends up to the banks of the Mekong and the borders with Laos and Cambodia, is undoubtedly the nation's least visited region. But that does not mean that it holds no interest for visitors – far from it. A thousand years ago the powerful Khmer empire ruled over the entire area, and its legacy of a considerable archeological heritage recalls the greatness and magnificence of Angkor, the ancient Khmer capital in Cambodia.

Furthermore, recent digs have confirmed the theory that 5000 years ago the plateau was the site of a flourishing Bronze Age civilization.

The Northeast, also known as I-San, has a population of over 20 million, descended from the people who arrived there long ago from Laos, Vietnam and Cambodia. They practice agriculture. Centuries of isolation from the rest of the country has allowed the I-San's population to preserve a unique culture and lifestyle, reflected in their exotic festivals and their dialects which derive from the ancient languages of Laos and Cambodia.

The city of Nakhon Ratchasima, better known as Khorat, is situated around 160 miles (260 km) northeast of Bangkok; it is considered the "Gate to the I-San" and is the ideal base for excursions to the surrounding archeological sites. The first among these is the Phimai site (37 miles/60 km northeast of Khorat); it is the largest, with a series of monuments arranged scenically around the main temple. This is a typical 11th-century *prasat hin* (stone castle), one of the best examples of Khmer architecture ever discovered outside Cambodia. Smaller but perhaps even more evocative is Prasat Phanom Wan, also near Khorat; unlike the others and despite the fact that it is in ruins, it is still used today by the monks of a nearby monastery.

Prasat Phanom Rung, south of Buri Ram and very near the Cambodian border, is the most spectacular temple, a monument to the power of the Khmer. The sanctuary was built on top of a hill and an imposing stone staircase leads up to a façade decorated with fine bas-reliefs. At the foot of the hill stand the ruins of another temple, Prasat Muang Tam, which is the least well preserved of all the temples but has a special charm thanks to the tranquillity of the surrounding landscape. Unspoilt and undiscovered, the I-San is certainly not lacking in attractions.

These include the university town of Khon Kaen, famous for its fine silk; Surin, where a great elephant gathering is held every November, drawing spectators and the curious from all over Thailand and beyond; and also Ubon Ratchathani, location of an imposing Buddhist Rain Retreat, preceded by a charming Festival of Candles.

218 left The solitude of this absorbed countrywoman of the I-San evokes the special quality of this isolated but fascinating area.

218 right The vast, barren plain of the I-San has been the focus of most of King Rama IX's efforts to improve farming techniques.

218-219 The inhabitants of the I-San mostly have distant Cambodian or Laotian origins, so the local dialects differ noticeably from the standard Thai language.

219 top left and right Phimai, north of Khorat (Nakhon Ratchasima), still has some remarkable ruins of the prasat hin, the magnificent Khmer "stone palaces."

220-221 The ruins of the Prasat Hin Phimai temple at Pimai are one of the best examples of Khmer religious architecture to have been built outside Cambodia.

INDEX

PHOTO CREDITS

224 *The focal point of spirituality in ancient*
Sukhothai, this statue of the Buddha in
Wat Mahathat is mirrored in the water of the
canal which surrounds the complex.